Isola di
Murano

Isola di
San Michele

Laguna
Veneta

Canale delle Fondamente Nuove

S. S. Giovanni
e Paolo

S. Francesco
d. Vigna

S. Maria
Formosa

S. Lorenzo

CASTELLO

Canale di Porta Nuova

Basilica di
S. Marco

Ponte dei
Sospiri

Darsena
Grande

S. Pietro
di Castello

1

Palazzo
Ducale

Arsenale

Isola di
S. Pietro

8 **5**

6

Museo
Storico
Navale

Canale di
San Marco

Monumento a Garibaldi

Darsena
di
Sant'Elena

S. Giorgio
Maggiore

Biennale

Isola di
San Giorgio
Maggiore

Darsena di Sant'

Teatro Verde

Rio dei Giardini

Le Zitelle

QUARTIERE
S. ELENA

Isola di
Sant'Elena

INSIGHT GUIDES

VENICE
Step by Step

APA PUBLICATIONS L

Part of the Langenscheidt Publishing Group

CONTENTS

Introduction

Overview

Walks and Tours

Directory

Credits and Index

ABOUT THIS BOOK

This *Step by Step Guide* has been produced by the editors of Insight Guides, whose books have set the standard for visual travel guides since 1970. With top-quality photography and authoritative recommendations, this guidebook brings you the very best of Venice in a series of 14 tailor-made tours.

WALKS AND TOURS

The tours in the book provide something to suit all budgets, tastes and trip lengths. As well as covering Venice's many classic attractions, the routes also track lesser-known sights and up-and-coming areas. The tours embrace a range of interests, so whether you are a foodie, an architecture enthusiast, an art fan, a film buff or have children to entertain, you will find an option to suit you.

We strongly recommend that you read the whole of a tour before setting out. This should help you to familiarise yourself with the route and enable you to plan where to stop for refreshments – options for this are given in the blue 'Food and Drink' boxes, which are recog-

nisable by the knife-and-fork sign, on most pages.

For our pick of the walks by theme, consult Recommended Tours For... *(see pp.6–7).*

OVERVIEW

The tours are set in context by this introductory section, giving an overview of the city to set the scene, plus background information on food, drink, shopping and culture. A succinct history timeline in this chapter highlights the key events that have shaped Venice over the centuries.

DIRECTORY

Also supporting the tours is a Directory chapter, comprising a user-friendly, clearly organised A–Z of practical information, our pick of where to stay while you are in the city, nightlife listings and select restaurant recommendations; these eateries complement the more low-key cafés and restaurants that feature within the tours themselves, and are intended to offer a wider choice for evening dining.

Above from top: highlights of Venice: Venetian flag; Grand Canal; Carnival masks; gondolas; pretty backstreets.

The Authors

Lisa Gerard-Sharp revised this edition and contributed to the original book. Lisa is an award-winning travel writer and Italy specialist who has written numerous Insight Guides (including CityGuide Venice) as well as contributing to UK national newspapers, magazines and television. Since working as a TV editor in Rome, Lisa has spent extensive research periods in Venice, with recent reportage for *National Geographic Traveller* winning her a 'best magazine-writer' award. Many tours in this book were originally conceived by Italy specialist **Susie Boulton**, who has travelled extensively in the country for more than 25 years, and contributed to many Insight titles. In the first edition of this book, the tours were expanded by **Jessica Stewart**, a history of art graduate based in Italy.

Margin Tips
Shopping tips, historical facts, handy hints and information on activities help visitors to make the most of their time in Venice.

Feature Boxes
Notable topics are highlighted in these special boxes.

Key Facts Box
This box gives details of the distance covered on the tour, plus an estimate of how long it should take. It also states where the route starts and finishes, and gives key travel information such as which days are best to do the route or handy transport tips.

Route Map
Detailed cartography shows the itinerary clearly plotted with numbered dots. For more detailed mapping, see the pull-out map slotted inside the back cover.

Footers
Look here for the tour name, a map reference and the main attraction on the double-page.

Food and Drink
Recommendations of where to stop for refreshment are given in these boxes. The numbers prior to each restaurant/café name link to references in the main text. Restaurants in the Food and Drink boxes are plotted on the maps.

The € signs at the end of each entry reflect the approximate cost of a two-course meal for one, with a glass of house wine. These should be seen as a guide only. Price ranges, also quoted on the inside back flap for easy reference, are:

€€€€	85 euros and above
€€€	55–85 euros
€€	25–55 euros
€	25 euros and under

ARCHITECTURE FANS

City highlights include St Mark's unrestrainedly decorative basilica (walk 1), Venetian Gothic palaces, such as the Ca' d'Oro, on the Grand Canal (tour 2), classical Venetian grandeur at the Gesuati (walk 7), the Palladian masterpieces of San Giorgio Maggiore and Il Redentore (tour 8) and the magnificent Gothic church of the Frari (walk 9).

RECOMMENDED TOURS FOR...

ART BUFFS

Spend a few hours in the Accademia (tour 3), visit the Guggenheim and Punta della Dogana contemporary art collections (walk 7), or marvel at masterpieces by Tintoretto, Titian and Bellini on walk 9. On walk 5 the Querini-Stampalia is a lovely little gallery of Venetian art.

CHILDREN

Head up the bell tower in Piazza San Marco (walk 1); take a boat trip on the Grand Canal (tour 2); sample mouthwatering ice creams on the Zattere (tour 7); have fun on the beach or on a bike around the Lido (tour 13).

ESCAPING THE CROWDS

It may be jam-packed around Piazza San Marco, but just off the beaten track, in Castello (walk 5), Cannaregio (walk 11), and even in the Giudecca (tour 8), you should find peace and quiet. For real tranquillity, visit the cemetery island of San Michele (tour 11) or Mazzorbo (tour 12).

FILM FANS

Admire the Grand Canal palaces (tour 2) that featured in *Casino Royale*, pay homage to Visconti's *Death in Venice* at the Lido's seafront (tour 13) and visit Castello (walks 5 and 6) and San Polo (walk 9), where parts of *Don't Look Now* were filmed.

FOODIES

Foodies are well advised to head off the beaten track to discover authentic Venetian bars and restaurants. Try Cannaregio (walk 11) for traditional *bacari;* the Rialto (walk 10) for authentic old bars and cosy inns; and around the quiet squares and backstreets in Castello, San Polo or Dorsoduro for funkier, reinvented *bacari* (walks 5, 6, 7 and 9).

LOVERS OF LITERATURE

Marcel Proust pondered the passing of time at Caffè Florian (walk 1), Lord Byron occupied several palaces on the Grand Canal (tour 2) while Ernest Hemingway was a regular at Harry's Bar (walk 4) and the islands (tour 12). For home-grown writers, visit the Casa Goldoni (walk 9), birthplace of the 18th-century Venetian playwright.

MUSIC LOVERS

After twice being reduced to ashes by fire, La Fenice has been restored and can be toured (walk 4). Look out for classical concerts in the Scuole (walk 9), in churches: La Salute (tour 7), the Frari (walk 9), Santa Maria Formosa (walk 5) and La Pietà *(see p.22);* and palaces, including the Ca' Rezzonico (tour 2) and Querini-Stampalia (walk 5).

ROMANTICS

Lap up the Grand Canal on a late-night ferry (tour 2); have dinner on a lagoon island: Venissa on Burano (tour 12); take an atmospheric gondola ride with the only female gondolier *(see p.52);* or simply fall for Venice in the winter mists.

SHOPPERS

The area west of San Marco (walk 4) is where to buy designer wares, but for typically Venetian crafts, try Santa Croce (walk 9), especially for masks; also try Cannaregio (tour 11) for crafts, Murano (tour 12) for glass; and the Rialto (walk 10) for food.

OVERVIEW

An overview of Venice's geography, customs and culture,
plus illuminating background information on food and drink,
shopping, carnival, culture and history.

INTRODUCTION

More like a stage set than a city, Venice has captivated visitors for centuries. La Serenissima is one of the wonders of the world. It dazzles and mesmerises, but also bewilders. These walks reveal show-stopping sights, secret corners – and the elusive Venetians themselves.

Endlessly portrayed by writers, painters and philosophers, Venice is a canvas for every clichéd fantasy. Almost everyone who is anyone has been there. Even the cafés of Piazza San Marco are awash with famous ghosts. As a result, Venice can play cultural one-upmanship better than most cities. The Romantics were rewarded with a feeling of having come too late to a world too old. The Victorians saw

Below: transport, Venetian-style.

Venice as dying, while contemporary doom-mongers now seek to bury the city anew. Although entombment by the sea would show symmetry, this resilient city rejects such neat scenarios, with new life and vitality being pumped through its veins.

The only city in the world built entirely on water, Venice is no mere fantasy land, but a superior theme park that can uplift the spirit. You can sleep in Tchaikovsky's bed or wake up in cavernous apartments that once welcomed princes and doges, Henry James and Hemingway. For romance, you can literally walk in Casanova's footsteps; for Baroque passion, succumb to a Vivaldi concerto in Vivaldi's church, or savour the gondoliers' songs that inspired Verdi and Wagner. If feeling adventurous, explore the world of Marco Polo in his home city, bargain in the Rialto with latter-day merchants of Venice, or pick up the cobalt-blue cabbages that sent Elizabeth David into culinary raptures.

If feeling contemplative, you can ponder the passing of time with Proust's ghost in Caffè Florian. If fortunate, you can capture Canaletto's views with your camera or see Titian's painting in the church it was designed for. If gregarious, you can savour the gossip and Martinis

at Harry's Bar, Hemingway's favourite. The morbid can play roulette in Wagner's death chamber, now the city casino, or quietly contemplate death on Thomas Mann's Lido.

For more than a millennium, the Republic of Venice used all its power to repel unwelcome invaders. Today, one of the greatest ever maritime powers has become one of the greatest ever tourist attractions.

NAVIGATING THE CITY

Venice is divided into six *sestieri* (districts), with very different characters. This guide presents their particularities, outlines a vaporetto trip along the Grand Canal and transports you to the islands in the lagoon.

As well as encompassing the architectural glories, we unpick the city neighbourhoods, including an insider's take on lesser-known corners, from bohemian bars to authentic crafts shops. Despite its watery character, Venice is made for walking: you can mostly weave your way around on foot, with brief forays on ferries that circle the city or whisk you to the outer reaches of the lagoon.

Pounding the Streets

Venice is a magical city to explore on foot. Leave behind the San Marco crowds and you soon find yourself in a warren of narrow alleys *(calli)*, moody canals and secret *campi* (squares). Wherever you go there are waterfront cafés, or tiny *bacari* (bars), ideal for a prosecco and a plate of seafood tapas.

NEIGHBOURHOODS

No matter your intention, you are inexorably drawn back to Piazza San Marco, directed by the bossy yellow *'per San Marco'* signs that mark the main thoroughfares. It is no hardship to return. The beautifully proportioned square that Napoleon termed 'the finest drawing room in Europe' is home to the great Basilica, the Doge's Palace and gracious cafés.

Castello, San Polo and Santa Croce

To the north and east of San Marco lies Castello, the largest *sestiere*, with monumental Venice gradually giving way to domestic Venice, as dark alleys open onto bright, bustling squares. The area is home to several major churches, as well as the Arsenale, the great military and naval complex founded in the 12th century, and the Biennale gardens, home to the contemporary art and architecture shows that give Venice a modern edge.

San Polo and Santa Croce are adjoining districts that encompass the labyrinthine Rialto market, with its boisterous bars, and the iconic Rialto Bridge that, with St Mark's, is the city's mercantile heart and great pulsating hub. Nearby is the Frari, the greatest of all Venetian Gothic churches.

Cannaregio and Dorsoduro

Cannaregio offers a slice of everyday Venice, from domestic vignettes of washing draped above decrepit palaces to lovely churches on back canals, culminating in the haunting Jewish

Above from far left: San Giorgio Maggiore church at dusk; Carnival reveller; St Mark's Basilica.

Above: lion of St Mark; San Marco sculpture; view of St Mark's from the island of San Giorgio Maggiore.

Venice in Peril
According to Anna
Somers Cocks of
Venice in Peril, 'In St
Mark's, the humidity is
beginning to destroy
the Byzantine mosaics
in the atrium. The
MOSE mobile barrier
will gain us a bit of
time but we need to
show more foresight
and come up with a
strategy to safeguard
Venice's future.'
Controversially, the
international heritage
body advocates
charging visitors €10
to visit Venice.

Below: The Rialto

Ghetto. Chic Dorsoduro is the artiest *sestiere*, with beguiling walks along the Zattere quayside, and bohemian backwaters counterpointed by the grandstanding art and architecture of La Salute basilica, the Accademia gallery and the Guggenheim collection of modern art.

Islands of the Lagoon

Frequent ferries make the mysterious islands easy to reach. Murano is famous for glassmaking, Burano for colourful fishermen's cottages, and Torcello for its cathedral, the oldest monument in the lagoon. Giudecca, an island undergoing a rebirth, is home to Il Redentore church, a Palladian masterpiece, and to glamorous hotels and good-value *trattorie*. San Giorgio Maggiore is the site of a famous Benedictine monastery; while the Lido, a long strip of land between the city and the Adriatic, glories in its role as a superior film set.

VENICE IN PERIL

The biggest watery threats to Venice are *acqua alta* (high water) and wave damage from boats to the foundations of buildings. In winter, duckboards are a familiar sight in low-lying Piazza San Marco. Work is underway on the controversial MOSE project, the mobile flood barriers that will close off the lagoon during the high tides, but at best it is only a partial solution as, according to Venice in Peril, high water levels are already damaging the building fabric. Controversially, cruise ships are still allowed into the lagoon. Just as crucially, Venice may be mired in its glorious past, with Gothic palaces galore, but it needs to retain its population if it is to stave off its fate as a theme park.

Venice's resident population has shrunk to 59,000, leaving the Venetians an endangered species. In a challenge to the city authorities, a pharmacy by the Rialto Bridge displays a monitor showing the (regularly updated) falling resident figures. Not only do visitors far outnumber locals, but the resident ageing population is being pushed out by rocketing rents and house prices, and all the extra costs that living in a lagoon city entails. Architect and broadcaster Francesco da Mosto worries whether his children will be the last generation to go to school in Venice. Chef Enrica Rocca mocks her neighbourhood as a place in which 'you can buy a mask more easily than milk'. Designer and activist Michela Scibilla says her son can't help viewing the hordes of visitors to his city in the same light as aliens, extra-terrestrial beings. Only the hoteliers are happy. Local people are determined not to live in Disneyland.

THE VENETIANS

Venetian residents are struggling to survive in a city dedicated to other people's dreams. But they are fighting back, carving out a space for themselves. Michela Scibilla and her 40 x Venezia pressure group are challenging the city to stop selling off its heritage. On Giudecca, gondola-maker 'Crea' continues to craft gondolas but is helping to save the boatyard by creating a new crafts centre – for ancient crafts.

All this despite the fact that the character of the city 'is old, conservative and resistant to change. Here in the historic centre we lack the capacity for renewal, or even the numbers required to effect a change', says Massimo Cacciari, the former mayor of Venice, speaking as ponderously and lugubriously as ever.

Yet the elusive Venetian spirit transcends such truisms, defies the simple arithmetic of the doom-mongers, and refuses to be confined by the strait-jacket of tourism. Cool, independent Venetians are nothing if not survivors.

Cacciari is sanguine about the future: 'If Venice has any vitality left, it will seize the moment. If it is dead in human terms, it will die. After all, Babylon, Alexandria and Rome have all died.' While at odds with the Venetians' positive approach to life, this view echoes their classic philosophical detachment. As such, the mayor shows himself to be a contradictory character, and that is the mark of a true Venetian.

Venetian Addresses
Addresses can be bewildering, labelled by just the street number and neighbourhood: if in doubt, ask the name of the closest parish church; this is more helpful than the postal address. But still expect to get lost in this labyrinthine city. This geographical oddness is captured in Venetian dialect, with street names providing clues to the nature of the city. Familiarity with these terms will help in identifying places on your trails through the confusing backwaters. Venetian spelling is variable, so expect alternative versions. For a list, see p.102.

Meet the Venetians

Don't day-dream your way through the city but drift a while with ordinary Venetians, and support sustainable tourism. Whether it's staying in a B&B, attending a Baroque recital, or doing a Venetian rowing course, you are helping Venice survive, with all its crafts and ancient skills, and getting to know Venetians at the same time. Before buying that cheap Taiwanese mask, call into a real craft shop and feel the difference. Rent a rococo costume from Atelier Nicolao. Pick up some lion-encrusted stationery at Gianni Basso. Glide into the lagoon and be a gondolier for a day with Row Venice. Book a ceramics workshop through the Venetian Club. Chat to bookbinder Paolo Olbi and caress the hand-tooled notebooks that caught Johnny Depp's attention. Venice could even change your life: Paolo Olbi is looking for an apprentice.

FOOD AND DRINK

The best places to head for when you're hungry in Venice are the authentic bars and everyday inns, known as bacari. *This is where local people graze, in both new-wave and traditional bars, and usually with a prosecco or spritz to hand.*

Table tips

Beyond St Mark's, a number of individualistic restaurants have opened, and late-night dining has become more widespread; only Sundays can be tricky, with better restaurants often closed. Reservations at restaurants are essential, especially at weekends. As the best eateries are often both cramped and coveted by Venetians, call a day or so in advance to assure yourself a table. Also, remember most restaurants close between lunch and dinner, so if you are hungry between these times, pop into a bar for some *tramezzini* (little triangular sandwiches on white bread).

Food critics tend to damn Venetian food as overpriced and underachieving, but you can eat well if you choose wisely. Even so, the difficulty of transporting fresh produce generally adds considerably to restaurant prices. Yet for seafood lovers, the cuisine can be memorable, with soft-shelled lagoon crabs, plump red mullet, pasta with lobster or black and pungent with cuttlefish ink.

VENETIAN CUISINE

According to top British chef and Italophile Alastair Little, 'The city's cosmopolitan past and superb produce imported from the Veneto have given rise to Italy's most eclectic and subtle style of cookery.' Like the Sicilians, the Venetians absorbed culinary ideas from the Arabs; they also raided Byzantium and, according to the Middle Eastern cookery writer Claudia Roden, translated it into their own simple style: 'If you could see the fish come in live at dawn in barges on the Grand Canal straight onto the market stalls, you would understand why all they want to do is lightly fry, poach or grill it.'

Culinary Melting Pot

As the hub of a cosmopolitan trading empire, Venice was bristling with foreign communities – Arabs, Armenians, Greeks, Jews and Turks – each with its own distinctive culinary tradition. Venetian trading posts in the Levant gave the city access to spices, the secret of subtle Venetian cookery. Pimiento, turmeric, ginger, cinnamon, cumin, cloves, nutmeg, saffron and vanilla show the oriental influences; pine nuts, raisins, almonds and pistachios also play their their part. Drogheria Mascari (on Ruga degli Spezieri) remains as the last of the scented spice shops that once dotted the Rialto.

Reflecting later conquests of Venice, these exotic ingredients are enriched with a dash of French or Austrian cuisine. From the end of the 18th century, French influence meant that oriental spices were supplanted by Mediterranean herbs.

The French brioche was added to the breakfast repertoire, as was the Turkish *crescente* (literally a crescent). The appearance of the croissant dates back to the Turkish defeat at the walls of Vienna in 1683. The Austrian conquest may have left Venice with a bitter taste in its mouth, but it also left the city with a keen appetite for the conquerors' apple strudel and *krapfen* (doughnuts).

Eclectic Tastes

A classic Middle Eastern-inspired dish is *sarde in saor*, tart sardines marinated in standard Venetian sauce. *Melanzane in saor*, made with aubergines, is the vegetarian version. *Saor* means savoury or tasty, and is a spicy sauce made with permutations of onions, raisins, vinegar, pine nuts and olive oil. *Riso* (rice), rather than pasta, predominates, prized for its versatility ever since its introduction by the Arabs. Creamy Venetian risotto offers endless possibilities, flavoured with spring vegetables, meat, game or fish. *Risi e bisi* (rice and peas) is a thick soup blended with ham, celery and onion. Equally delicious are the seasonal risottos, cooked with asparagus tips, artichoke hearts, fennel, courgettes or pumpkins. An oriental variant involves sultanas and pine nuts.

Fish Dishes

Most local menus come from the Adriatic but inland fishing also occurs in *valli*, fish farms in the lagoon, mainly for grey mullet *(cefalu)* and eel *(anguilla)*. It is hard to better *antipasti di frutti di mare*, a feast of simply cooked shellfish and molluscs, dressed with olive oil and lemon juice; prawns and soft-shelled crabs vie with baby octopus and squid. A trademark dish is cuttlefish risotto, served black and pungent with ink, or *granseola*, spider crab, boiled and then dressed simply in lemon and oil. Another staple is *baccalà*, dried salt cod, prepared with milk and herbs or parmesan and parsley, and served in countless ways on *crostini*.

In Venice, fish predominates, but offal is also favoured, particularly in *fegato alla veneziana*, calves' liver sliced into ribbons and cooked with parsley and onions.

DESSERTS

Save room for pudding, because Venetian biscuits, cakes and desserts are excellent, flavoured with exotic spices ever since the discovery of cinnamon and nutmeg. The Venetians introduced cane sugar to Europe, and have retained their sweet tooth. Spicy sweets are popular, including *fritelle di zucca*, sweet pumpkin doughnut served hot, while the best ices can be found in *gelaterie* such as Grom on Campo San Barnaba, or Nico on the Zattere.

Cicchetti

Some of the most common *cicchetti* (Venetian tapas) are *polpette* (spicy meatballs), *carciofini* (artichoke hearts), *crostini* with grilled vegetables, *baccalà mantecato* (salt cod on polenta), *seppie roste* (grilled cuttlefish) and anchovy nibbles. Keep track of what you eat, as you'll be charged per piece (prices start from €2).

Above: fresh produce in markets at the Rialto.

WHERE TO EAT

Venetian celebrity chef Enrica Rocca praises her home cuisine but also advises visitors to splash out on somewhere exceptional such as Ristorante Quadri, a current favourite: 'My philosophy of life is to eat one great meal and live on *cicchetti* for the rest of the time,' she teases. San Marco and Castello are home to some of the city's most prestigious restaurants, but privacy is rare in these goldfish-bowl settings. Further away from St Mark's, dining experiences tend to be more authentic, and more affordable. Try Cannaregio and the Rialto area for decent, well-priced meals. Not that visitors should ignore overtly glamorous spots; the Venetians patronise them too, including Caffè Quadri and Harry's Bar.

Styles of Restaurant

Until recently, Venetian restaurants opted for cool, 18th-century elegance, or the exposed beams and copper pots that spell rustic gentility. Yet individualistic, even contemporary, inns now abound, whether tucked under pergolas or spilling onto terraces and courtyards. Reservations are required for the grander restaurants, which tend to be fairly dressy affairs, especially in the more elegant hotels. The opposite is true of the *bacari*, the traditional wine bars, where you could dress as a fishmonger if you felt like it.

More up-market places are termed *ristoranti*, but may be called *osterie* (inns) if they focus on homely food in an intimate or rustic setting. To confuse the issue, some inns have bars that act like traditional *bacari*, offering a full sit-down meal at a table, or quicker, cheaper nibbles at the bar. Even so, the distinction between bars and restaurants is somewhat blurred, as most *bacari* also serve food, typically the Venetian equivalent of tapas, known as *cicchetti (see margin, left)*. To eat *cicchetti e l'ombra*, a snack and a glass of wine, is a Venetian tradition.

DRINKS

Wine

The Veneto produces a number of superior (DOC) wines, from the fruity, garnet-red Bardolino to the less prestigious Valpolicella. Venetians drink far more white wine than red, partly through habit, partly because it is a better accompaniment to seafood.

Soave, which comes from vineyards dotted along the eastern shores of Lake Garda, can be rather bland. Dry whites from the Veneto and Friuli go particularly well with seafood dishes, as does the first vintage of Venetian wine from Venissa *(see Tour 12)*, a vineyard that has recently been reclaimed from the lagoon.

Cocktails

Venice is noted for its cocktails, especially the Bellini, a peach-and-prosecco *aperitivo* created in the 1930s in Harry's Bar *(see p.116)*. Prosecco, the sparkling wine from the Veneto, makes a fine aperitif, whether drunk dry *(secco)* or medium sweet *(amabile)*. It is drunk at

the drop of a hat but is still distinctive enough for you to recognise a good one after a few days in Venice.

But to really look like a Venetian, risk the lurid orange cocktail known as a spritz (pronounced 'spriss' in Venetian dialect). The bright orange drink was introduced under Austrian rule (named after the introduction of 'selzer', fizzy soda water) and soon became a firm favourite. It consists of roughly equal parts of dry white wine, soda water and a herb-based aperitif, usually Campari, Cynar or Aperol, and garnished with a twist of lemon or an olive. Ask for a *spritz al bitter* for a stronger, less cloying taste. The spritz may be an acquired taste, but once acquired, it's the clearest sign that you've fallen for Venice.

Where to Drink

Not much changes in the historic cafés close to San Marco, where coffee has been drunk for centuries and post-prandial grappas downed since the days of the doges. Yet just beyond San Marco are serious wine bars *(enoteche)*, where tastings are the main draw. Over the last few years, there has been a trend for new wine bars, too, including cool reinterpretations of the *bacaro*; a few, such as Caffè Centrale, are sleek designer gastro-bars that would be at home in Manhattan – apart from the gondola moored by the back door. Even a number of once-staid hotel cocktail bars have been relaunched as cool lounge bars. As a result, Venetian bar culture is far broader than piano bars in sophisticated hotels *(see Nightlife)*.

Above from far left: enjoying a drink outside a *bacaro*; spaghetti *alla vongole*, (with clams).

Cocktail Hour

Between 6pm and 8pm is 'cocktail time', a Venetian ritual. At this time, local people can be seen sipping wine or classic cocktails both in chic cafés and old-fashioned neighbourhood bars or *bacari*.

Below: romantic al fresco dining .

SHOPPING

For sustainable shopping, seek out traditional Venetian crafts, from leather-bound notebooks to ceramics, luxury fabrics and marbled paper – but buy Murano glassware and masks only where the provenance is guaranteed.

Above: Murano glass door knobs.

Opening Hours
Many stores keep opening hours of 9:30/10am to 12.30/1pm, then 3.30/4pm until 7.30/8pm, so plan your shopping accordingly. Many smaller boutiques also close for the day on either Sunday or Monday. Some stores close either in August for the summer vacation or in January, when fewer visitors are in the city. Larger shops and department stores, especially near San Marco, tend, however, to stay open all day.

To enjoy the excitement of finding something truly Venetian, you need curiosity, conviction and a sense of adventure. Craft shopping is an intimate experience, a secret glimpse of Venetians at their best. And, if the costs are quite high, remember that by supporting these ancient crafts, you are also supporting the city itself.

MASKS AND COSTUMES

If you want to buy a Venetian mask, always check what it is made of and ask the seller to tell you how it fits into the Venetian tradition – whether it is a character from the *commedia dell'arte (see p.69)*, for instance. Just off Campo Santa Maria Formosa, the archetypal Venetian square, Papier Machè is an authentic mask shop (Calle Lunga S. Maria Formosa; tel: 041-522 9995). Here, over 30 years ago, Stefano Gottardo helped relaunch Carnival and the moribund craft of mask-decorating. Since then, his distinctive one-off pieces have been sought after as design objects and featured in Stanley Kubrick's orgiastic *Eyes Wide Shut*. Also in the Castello district is Ca' del Sol, an appealing mask shop in the quiet canals behind San Zaccaria (Fondamenta del Osmarin, Castello 4964; tel: 041-528 5549). Mondonovo

is one of the most creative mask-makers (Rio Terrà Canal, off Campo Santa Margherita, Dorsoduro 3063; tel: 041-528 7344). Also in Dorsoduro, Ca' Macana (Calle della Botteghe, Dorsoduro 3172, tel: 041-277 6142), offers mask-making courses.

TEXTILES

Venice is well known for Fortuny fabrics – silks and velvets, whether plain or gloriously patterned. Venetia Studium (Calle Larga XXII Marzo, San Marco 2403; tel: 041-522 9281) produces exclusive fabrics, including Fortuny designs, from scarves to cushion covers to lamps, as well as soft furnishings. Another big name in fabrics is Bevilacqua (Ponte della Canonica, San Marco 337b; tel: 041-528 7581; also at San Marco 2520; tel: 041-241 0662), which has been producing velvets and brocades since 1875; many are still produced on traditional 18th-century wooden looms.

Jesurum (Fondamenta della Sensa, Cannaregio 3219; tel: 041-524 2540) has been selling princely household linen, including embroidered sheets, since 1870. Frette (Calle Larga XXII Marzo, San Marco 2070a; tel: 041-522 4914) sells fine linens, exquisite sheets, cushions and bathrobes.

MARBLED PAPER

Between San Marco and the Rialto are shops selling marbled paper. Called *legatoria* or 'bookbinding', this ancient craft gives paper a decorative marbled veneer and is used nowadays for photo albums, writing cases, greeting cards, diaries and notebooks. Good stockists include Cartavenezia (Calle Longa, Santa Croce 2125; tel: 041-524 1283) and Paoli Olbi (Campo Santa Maria Nova, Cannaregio 6061; tel: 041-523 7655). Paolo Olbi himself is as much a Venetian gem as the bejewelled Miracoli church around the corner. The master-craftsman's shop is stuffed with leather-bound notebooks studded with Venetian motifs, such as the Lion of St Mark.

MURANO GLASS

It's fashionable to mock Murano glass, but the best pieces are works of art, from show-stopping chandeliers to sophisticated sculpture signed by great Italian artists and designers. One of the most prestigious contemporary glass-makers is Venini (shop on Piazzetta Leoncini, San Marco 314, with factory and showrooms on Fondamenta Vetrai 50, Murano; tel: 041-273 7211). Venini has created artworks with such illus-trious talents as Giò Ponti, Gae Aulenti and Ettore Sottsass. As the superior glassmakers mostly have showrooms clustered around San Marco, you could easily get a feel for the glassware on Murano, and see how it's made, before buying in Venice itself. Other illustrious

names include Barovier e Toso (Fondamenta Vetrai 28, Murano; tel: 041-739 049) and Pauly & C (both at San Marco and on Fondamenta Vetrai 43, Murano; tel: 041-736 843). In the Dorsoduro district, Napé Gallery sells collectors' pieces even Venetians buy, designed by virtuoso glassmakers, as well as quirky, everyday drinking glasses known as *goti* (tel: 041-296 0734, http://www.murano900.com).

BOOKS AND PRINTS

Bookworms should head for Mondadori (Salizzada San Moise, San Marco 1345), a cool, central late-night bookshop, gallery and multimedia centre, with Bacaro, an equally hip bar, attached. For prints, La Stamperia del Ghetto (Calle del Ghetto Vecchio, Cannaregio 1185a; tel: 041-275 0200) includes general and Jewish themes. Gianni Basso (Calle del Fumo, Cannaregio 5306; tel: 041-523 4681) churns out business cards, bookplates and stationery for clients all over the world in his tiny printing studio.

DESIGNER GOODS

Venice abounds in designer booty but prices tend to be higher than on the mainland. The most elegant boutiques are on Calle Vallaresso, Salizzada San Moisè, the Frezzeria and Calle Larga XXII Marzo, west of San Marco. But far more fun is the classic fabric and haberdashery quarter known as the Mercerie, a maze of alleys that winds between San Marco and the Rialto.

Above from far left: scarves, masks and Murano glassware for sale.

Hip Dorsoduro
Head to Dorsoduro for some of the most trendy and artistic boutiques in the city. As many artists live in the area, this *sestiere* is bursting with contemporary art galleries, printmakers and designers.

Glass advice
Remember that Murano glass can be found both on the island and in numerous *ateliers* in the lagoon. Resist the hard sell before you know what you like. If you're not sure of your taste, slip into the new glass museum on the monastic island of San Giorgio, across the water from St Mark's Square *(Tour 8)*. Set in Fondazione Cini, the Stanze del Vetro is dedicated to 20th-century and contemporary glass, and opens with an exhibition of glass designed by architect Carlo Scarpa for Venini in the 1930s.

CARNIVAL

Venice Carnival is supreme self-indulgence, a giddy round of masked balls, parading along the waterfront, and private parties promising romance – a 'farewell to the flesh' that captivates the city in the run up to Shrove Tuesday

Above from left: masked revellers strike a pose; masks for sale.

Buying a Mask
If you want to buy a mask, it is worth visiting one of the traditional made-to-measure mask shops, where they can whip up anything from a brightly coloured festive Harlequin to a Medusa wreathed in snakes. The most traditional masks are made of leather *(in cuoio)* or papier mâché *(in cartapesta)*, with modern creations worked in ceramics or covered with luxurious fabrics. Leather masks are the hardest to fashion, while hand-held masks make striking wall decorations. (If you want inspiration for historically authentic carnival costumes, study Pietro Longhi's exquisite carnival paintings, in the Ca' Rezzonico; *see p.39*.)

It is fashionable to mock the carnival as a commercial fabrication, but its roots extend deep into the Venetian psyche. The city has an instinctive love of spectacle and dressing up, dating from the glory days of the Republic. Carnival reaches back to medieval times and represents a cavalcade of Venetian history, tracing political and military events, factional rivalries and defeats.

The Venetian carnival is also the inheritor of a rich folk tradition, linked to the winter solstice. According to pagan rites, winter was a force to be overcome, with the sun persuaded to return by a show of life at its most vital.

Christianity gave the carnival new significance: *carne vale*, the Latin for 'farewell to meat', meant a last gasp, particularly on Mardi Gras (Fat Tuesday), before the start of the rigorous Lenten period, marked by abstinence from pleasures of the flesh.

In the past, the Venetian carnival was something of a movable feast, beginning as early as October or Christmas and lasting until Lent. In addition to masquerades, there were rope dancers, acrobats and fire-eaters who routinely displayed their skills on Piazza San Marco. The diarist John Evelyn visited Venice in 1645–6 and reported on 'the folly and madness of the carnival', from the bull-baiting and flinging of eggs to

the superb opera, the singing eunuch and a shooting incident with an enraged nobleman and his courtesan, whose gondola canoodling he had disturbed. During the 1751 carnival, everyone gathered to admire an exotic beast, the rhinoceros, captured in a famous painting by Longhi, which is now displayed in the Ca' Rezzonico *(see p.39)*.

When Napoleon conquered Venice in 1797, the carnival went the tragic way of the Venetian Republic. Although revived sporadically in the early part of the 20th century, it was only fully restored in 1979. The event was eagerly reclaimed by Venetians, with playful processions and masquerades.

CARNIVAL CAPERS

Thousands of masqueraders see in the carnival on Piazza San Marco. This event is followed by pantomime, operetta, parading and concerts in the city's *campi*. In an attempt to reclaim carnival, Venetians are shifting celebrations to the neighbourhoods, but the set-pieces and the crowds still congregate on St Mark's Square.

The high point is Shrove Tuesday, when revellers gather for a masked ball on Piazza San Marco before moving on to private parties, notably Il Ballo del Doge, the Doge's Ball, which takes place

in the Grand Canal Palazzo Pisani-Moretta. In the past, the midnight fasting bell would ring out from San Francesco della Vigna, signalling an end to licence and the onset of atonement. The end is signalled when the effigy of Carnival is burnt on Piazza San Marco.

CARNIVAL TODAY

Carnival has much to answer for: prices soar, and the city has more mask shops than butchers; fashion shoots and film crews swamp San Marco; cavorting crowds of motley Europeans dress as gondoliers and bosomy courtesans. Processions of doges, nuns and Casanovas swan past shimmering palaces. Yet despite the crowds and commercialism, this kitsch masquerade retains its magic.

Today's carnival plays homage to the lavish lifestyles of 18th-century Venice. Costumes currently in vogue extol the voluptuous femininity of 18th-century dress for both sexes. The classic costume of the 17th and 18th centuries was the *maschera nobile*, the patrician mask. The head was covered with a *bautá*, a black silk hood and lace cape, topped by a voluminous cloak *(tabarro)*, in black silk for the nobility and in red or grey for ordinary citizens. The *volto*, the white half-mask, covered the face, with the finishing touch provided by a black tricorn hat adorned with feathers. The most traditional masks hark back to Venetian history or the tradition of the *commedia dell'arte (see p.69)*.

Certainly, the Venetian love of disguise masks a desire to slip into a different skin. As Oscar Wilde said, 'A man only reveals himself when wearing a mask.' A mask also makes everyone equal. Masqueraders are addressed as *'sior maschera'* (masked gentleman) regardless of age, rank or even gender.

To don a stunning disguise, visit Atelier Nicolao, the most authentic costumier's (tel: 041-520 7051; www. nicolao.com). Choose a cloak and hand-crafted mask or hire a full costume and slip back into the era of Casanova.

Festivals
Chances are there will be some celebration during your stay. The festive year begins with Carnival, including the Doge's Ball (tel: 041-241 3802, www.ilballodeldoge.com); and celebrations in honour of the city's patron saint, St Mark (25 April). Venice also plays host to water festivals redolent of the pomp and pageantry of the Republic, beginning with the Vogalonga rowing marathon in May. The grandest water pageant is September's Historical Regatta. The calvacade of boats winds its way from the Giardini quarter to Ca' Foscari on the Grand Canal, where prizes are presented by dignitaries on a ceremonial barge. It is followed by a gondola race. Other key dates include the Feast of the Redeemer *(see p.64)*; the Film Festival *(see p.23 and p.87)*; the Art Biennale (held in September in odd years); and November's Festa della Madonna della Salute, giving thanks for the city's survival from the plague. *(For festival dates, see p.100).*

Masters of Disguise

Mask-makers had their own guild in medieval times, when a *mascheraio* (mask-maker) helped a secretive, stratified society run smoothly. Masks were a ploy for protecting the identity of pleasure-seeking Venetians, from secret gamblers to lascivious priests and un-virginal nuns. The *bautá*, the expressionless white mask, was the most common disguise. A *Columbina* (Columbine) is the elegant domino mask; more catlike and seductive is the *civetta* (flirt). Other masks are quite sinister, notably the Plague Doctor: a distinctive beaked nose and black gown, once worn as a protection against the plague. The elegant *maschera nobile* and *commedia dell'arte* masks are not the only authentic disguises. Masks ridiculing the Republic's enemies, such as a Moor or Turk, remain popular, but so too do creative masks, generally known as *fantasie*, or fantasy masks.

MUSIC AND OPERA

Outside the Film Festival, evening entertainment mostly takes the form of concerts and opera at La Fenice, a jewel of an opera house. Here we give the low-down on concerts, opera and music festivals.

Above from left: musician in the Piazza San Marco; legendary La Fenice.

Ears to the ground
Keep your ears open for concerts as you stroll around, and your eyes open for posters advertising them. For forthcoming performances, check: www.musicinvenice. com. For opera, classical music and big-name concerts, book through HelloVenezia, and the office on Piazzale Roma, tel: 041-24 24; www.hellovenezia. com. The Venice Jazz Festival takes place in July and sees such legends as Wynton Marsalis perform at La Fenice. That's in addition to outdoor jazz and occasional performances by rock stars (www.veneto jazz.com). Also consult the Venice tourist board, APT Venezia, tel: 041-529 8711; www. turismovenezia.it.

CONCERTS AND OPERA

Venetians are passionate about their classical music and proud of the fact that Vivaldi, Monteverdi and Wagner all lived in the city. It helps that concerts are often held in beautiful settings, such as churches, oratories, frescoed palaces and the *scuole* (charitable confraternity seats). What's more, Venice is spearheading Italy's Baroque music revival, with musicians playing on authentic period instruments.

Autumn spells the start of the classical music season, and the start of the opera season at the reopened La Fenice (Campo San Fantin, San Marco; tel: 041-786 511; www.teatrolafenice.it; *see p.47*). Performances also take place in the diminutive Teatro Malibran (Campiello Malibran, Cannaregio; tel: 041-786 6611), with ballet and concerts sometimes staged in Teatro Goldoni (www.teatrostabileveneto.it).

Confraternity Concerts

The Scuola Grande di San Teodoro (tel: 041-521 0294; www.imusiciveneziani. it) stages concerts in the confraternity house, with the singers and orchestra dressed in 18th-century costumes. Concerts are also held in the sumptuously decorated confraternity houses of the Scuola Grande di San Rocco (tel: 041-

523 4864; *see p.65*), the Scuola Grande dei Carmini (tel: 041-528 9420), the Scuola Grande di San Giovanni Evangelista, and the Ospedaletto. Many of the best performances are staged by the Accademia di San Rocco, a musical ensemble that presents Baroque recitals in traditional Venetian settings.

Church Concerts

One of the most popular concert churches is La Pietà (Riva degli Schiavoni), the lovely rococo church linked to Vivaldi. La Pietà is naturally a magnificent setting for the Venetian composer's work and for concerts of Baroque music in general.

If you ever dismissed Vivaldi as muzak, thanks to its misuse in so many commercial situations, do listen to the Interpreti Veneziani (tel: 041-277 0561; www.interpretiveneziani.com) performing in the deconsecrated Chiesa San Vidal.

Classical concerts are also held in the Gothic church of I Frari *(see p.66)*, in Tintoretto's church of Madonna dell'Orto *(see p.76)* and in La Salute *(see p.58)*. The Renaissance church of Santa Maria dei Miracoli *(see p.78)*, the Rialto market church of San Giacometto (tel: 041-426 6559; www.ensembleantonio-vivaldi.com) and the neighbourhood Santa Maria Formosa *(see p.52)* are also

evocative settings for concerts. On Piazza San Marco, the Ateneo di San Basso (tel: 041-528 2825; www.virtuoso divenezia.com) is the setting for concerts of works by Vivaldi and Mozart.

Palaces

Concerts are also staged in the city's greatest palaces, from Ca' Vendramin-Calergi (where the music is usually Wagner) to Ca' Rezzonico, under a Tiepolo ceiling, no less (generally 18th-century music; tel: 041-4273 0892; *see p.39*). The Fondazione Querini-Stampalia (tel: 041-523 4411; www.querini stampalia.it; *see p.52*) is a small gallery providing an intimate yet sumptuous setting for concerts every Friday and Saturday at 5pm and 7pm.

Another extraordinary venue is the Collegium Ducale (Palazzo delle Prigioni, Castello; tel: 041-988 155). Linked to the Doge's Palace by the Bridge of Sighs, these former prisons make a superb spot for opera and Baroque concerts. Palazzo Barbarigo-Minotto (Fondamenta Barbarigo o Duodo 2504, tel: +39 340 971 7272, www.musicapalazzo.com) is a magical experience, with arias from Verdi and Rossini performed in a series of palatial salons.

Outdoor Concerts and Opera

In summer, key squares in the Dorso-duro district are turned into open-air concert venues, including Campo Pisani, just off Campo Santo Stefano. The 1,500-seat Teatro Verde (tel: 041-528 9900; www.cini.it) on the island of San Giorgio Maggiore also makes a great setting for operatic performances. In September, the Venezia Suona festival (www.veneziasuona.it, in Italian) is a long weekend of concerts taking place in squares and on abandoned islands.

Set in Venice

Venice has been the backdrop to many films, including Michael Radford's *The Merchant of Venice*, with Al Pacino as Shylock; Nicolas Roeg's eerily impressive *Don't Look Now*, starring Julie Christie and Donald Sutherland; Luchino Visconti's *Death in Venice*, starring Dirk Bogarde; and Fellini's *Casanova*, starring Donald Sutherland. The well-travelled Mr Bond drives a gondola on land in *Moonraker* and has all kinds of Venetian adventures in *Casino Royale*. The *Tourist,* starring Angelina Jolie and Johnny Depp, did neither any favours but Venice, at least, came out of it well.

Venice Film Festival

Opera and other, mainly classical, musical forms predominate in Venice, but in terms of entertainment we must not forget the cinema. Although it does not have an indigenous film industry, the city is the home of the world's oldest film festival, founded by Mussolini in 1932. For 10 days in September Venice plays host to Hollywood and European stars, and, of course, the attendant paparazzi from all over the world. The festival is centred on the Lido *(see Tour 13)*, in the revamped Palazzo del Cinemà, built in 1930s triumphalist Fascistic style. To spot the celebrities, just stroll along the beach-side boulevard or splash out on a cocktail on the sea-view terrace of the Hotel Excelsior. The Bauer, Palazzina Grassi and Cipriani are favourite places to stay for the Hollywood set *(see pp.110–15)*. During the glitzy festival *(see p.87)*, films are shown in their original versions. In 2012 the festival's artistic director, Alberto Barbera, declared that he was advocating 'a slimmed down, more sober, less glitzy' version of the festival: it can't possibly last. For more details, see www.labiennale.org/en/cinema.

HISTORY: KEY DATES

From its foundation among stagnant marshes on the shores of the Adriatic to glory days as the most powerful city in the West, Venice has seen it all. Thereafter came occupation and flooding, and now the tourists invade.

FIRST SETTLEMENTS

421	Foundation of Venice on 25 March, Feast Day of St Mark.
452–568	Attila the Hun plunders the Veneto. Mass migrations take place from the mainland to Venice.
697	The first doge, Paolo Lucio Anafesto, is elected to office.
814	The population moves to the more easily defended Rivo Alto (Rialto). Venetian coins first minted. Work begins on the first Doge's Palace.

HEIGHT OF THE REPUBLIC

828	St Mark's body is taken from Alexandria to Venice.
1000	Venice controls the Adriatic coast.
1095–9	Venice joins the Crusades, providing ships and supplies for First Crusade to liberate the Holy Land.
1173	First Rialto Bridge begun.
1202–4	Fourth Crusade; the sack of Constantinople and Venetian conquest of Byzantium provide a springboard for the growth of the Venetian empire. Arsenale shipyards are created. Venice becomes a world power.
1309–10	Work begins on the present Doge's Palace. The Council of Ten is established as a check on individual power and a monitor of security.
1348–9	A plague outbreak kills half the people of Venice.
1453–4	Constantinople falls to the Turks; zenith of Venetian empire: Treviso, Bergamo, Ravenna, Friuli, Udine and Istria are all conquered.
1489	Cyprus is ceded to Venice by Queen Caterina Cornaro.
1508	League of Cambrai unites Europe against Venice. Titian's *Assumption* is hung in the Frari church.
1571	Battle of Lepanto, a decisive naval victory against the Turks.
1577	Veneto-born Andrea Palladio designs Il Redentore church.
1669	Loss of Crete, the last major Venetian colony, to the Turks.
1708	A harsh winter freezes the lagoon; Venetians can walk to the mainland.
1718	Venice surrenders Morea (Peloponnese) to the Turks, signalling the loss of its maritime empire.
1790	Opening of La Fenice opera house.

Marriage of the Sea La Sensa, the Ascension festival, celebrates Venice's Marriage with the Sea; this historic festival has been in place since 1000. Until the fall of the Republic, the doge would sail from San Marco to the Lido in the Bucintoro, the ceremonial state barge. With great pomp, a ring was cast into the Adriatic, symbolising Venice's sacred union with the sea. Today's re-enactment is a pale imitation; the water marathon that follows is more memorable: La Vogalonga (Long Row) races from St Mark's Basin to Burano before returning via the Grand Canal, and involves not just the city but a record number of rowers from abroad.

UNDER OCCUPATION

Above from far left: daily life in Venice in the 18th century, as captured by Canaletto; La Fenice after the fire in 1996.

1797	Fall of the Republic. Napoleon grants Venice to Austria.
1800	Papal conclave in Venice to elect a pope.
1805–14	Napoleonic rule reinstated.
1815–66	Under the terms of the Congress of Vienna, Austria occupies the city.
1846	Venice is joined to the mainland by a railway causeway.
1861	Vittorio Emanuele is crowned king of a united Italy.
1866	Venice is annexed to the Kingdom of Italy.

20TH CENTURY

1931	A road causeway connects city to mainland.
1945	British troops liberate the city from Nazi occupiers.
1960	Construction of the Marco Polo airport.
1966	The worst flood in Venetian history hits the city.
1979	The Venice Carnival is revived.
1988	First stage of the flood barrier is completed.
1996	Burning down of La Fenice opera house. The worst floods and *acqua alta* (high tides) since 1966.

21ST CENTURY

2003	The MOSE (Moses) mobile flood barrier is approved.
2004	La Fenice reopens after reconstruction, with *La Traviata*. Venice gets broadband via fibre-optic cables, dispensing with satellite dishes.
2008	The controversial Ponte Calatrava is constructed across the Grand Canal, linking the railway station with Piazzale Roma. On the vaporetto, the iMod, an electronic, rechargeable ticket, is introduced.
2009	After relaunching Palazzo Grassi as a showcase for contemporary art in 2005, French magnate François Pinault repeats his feat with the Punta della Dogana, opened in the former Customs House.
2011	The Bridge of Sighs is restored to former glory, after a five-year wait.
2012	Venice 'goes green' with the introduction of Alilaguna's silent, eco-friendly 'Energia' boats that link the Rialto with the airport. The MOSE mobile gates are installed across the Lido entrance to the lagoon. The new Art Heritage waterbus cruises the Grand Canal and stops at landing stages linked to the key museums. La Vogalonga (Long Row) water marathon attracts record numbers.
2013	The MOSE mobile barrier is extended to the remaining two entrances to the Venice lagoon.

WALKS AND TOURS

PIAZZA SAN MARCO

Piazza San Marco is the focus of Venetian life. Start with the splendours of the Basilica and the Doge's Palace, then saunter along the Riva degli Schiavoni, relax in a café and absorb the sublime views across the lagoon.

DISTANCE 1km (⅔ mile)
TIME A full day
START Basilica San Marco
END Torre dell' Orologio
POINTS TO NOTE

Booking a slot online at least two days before your visit means that you won't have to join a queue; contact ALATA on www.alata.it (no charge). Another way to avoid queuing is to check in a bag (no large bags or backpacks are allowed inside) at the Ateneo S. Basso (Calle S. Basso, by the Piazzetta dei Leoncini). You will be given a tag that can be taken to the guards and will allow you to skip the queue. To get the best views of the mosaics, visit when the Basilica is illuminated, from 11.30am–12.30pm daily. To avoid the crowds, go early morning or late after-noon, avoiding weekends if possible. Beware that visitors are usually herded through the Basilica and encouraged to spend no more than 10 minutes during a visit. Scantily dressed visitors, eg those wearing shorts or with uncovered shoulders, will be turned away. Bear in mind that, despite the limited walking on this tour, the crowds will make this an exhausting, intense day's exploration, so do take time to relax over lunch.

Acqua Alta

Deadly flooding known as *acqua alta* (high water) invades the low-lying piazza some 250 times a year. The building of a controversial new tidal barrier named MOSE (after the prophet Moses, who parted the waves) is well under way, and the mobile barriers should be in action by 2014. For now, whenever the square floods, duckboards are laid down so that people can cross without getting wet feet. It is a novelty for tourists, but a headache for the city authorities.

Piazza San Marco, famously dubbed 'the most elegant drawing room in Europe' by Napoleon, is the focal point of Venice. It is the only square in the city important enough to be called a piazza. For most of the day, it is the domain of tourists and street-sellers, but St Mark's belongs to the citizens as well as visitors. Venetians them-selves will drink at the grand cafés, even if they often save money by standing up. Before braving the hordes in the Basilica, consider splashing out on a coffee or prosecco at **Florian**, see ⑪①, prince of the city's coffee houses and haunt of such literary giants as Byron, Dickens, Proust and Guardi. Linger as long as you like, preferably alfresco, to admire one of the most often-praised squares in the world.

ST MARK'S BASILICA

The centrepiece of the square is the sumptuous **Basilica San Marco** ❶ (Piazza San Marco; tel: 041-522 5205; www.basilicasanmarco.it; daily 9.45am–5pm; charge only for Marciano Museum, Pala d'Oro and Treasury), the shrine of the Republic and symbol of Venetian glory. For once, the restored facade is free of scaffolding so revel in the view. Before joining the queue for the Basilica, take a close look at the

external sculpture, mosaics and the four horses above the central portal. These are replicas of the originals, which were looted from Constantinople during the Fourth Crusade. They were moved to the Marciano Museum inside the Basilica to protect them from pollution.

Myriad Mosaics

Of all the mosaics decorating the entrances and upper portals, the only original is *The Translation of the Body of the Saint* above the door on the far left. Look closely to see how the Basilica looked in the 13th century. The lower portal on the far right has a mosaic showing how the body of St Mark was taken from Alexandria, reputedly smuggled under slices of pork. Turbaned Muslims are showing their revulsion at the smell – the figure in the blue cloak is holding his nose.

The atrium mosaics are some of the finest in the Basilica: on the right **The Genesis Cupola** describes the *Creation of the World* in concentric circles, followed by scenes from the stories of Noah. Either side of the central portal are the oldest mosaics in the Basilica, *The Virgin with Apostles and Saints*.

Marciano Museum

Take the steep narrow steps up to the **Museo Marciano**, the gallery above the entrance portal. It is well worth the admission fee to see the original **bronze horses** and the views into the Basilica and over the Piazza. At first

Above from far left: the domes of the Basilica San Marco; gilded mosaic in the Basilica.

Above: Basilica door-knob; the Campanile.

Food and Drink

① CAFFÈ FLORIAN

Piazza San Marco; tel: 041-520 5641; Thur–Tue; €€

The renowned Florian is the place for a prosecco or a Venetian spritz in style, while drowning in dubious musical offerings, but Florian remains a Venetian institution and comes into its own during festivities such as the Carnival and regattas. You pay more when the band strikes up.

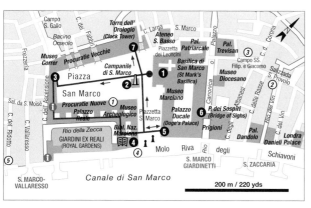

Pigeon Ban

You may notice a conspicuous absence of the famed pigeon-feed vendors in the piazza. They were banned by the city in 2008, as it was proved that the pigeon droppings were causing damage to the monuments. Anyone now seen feeding pigeons in the square faces a fine.

For Whom the Bell Tolls

During the Republic, each of the bells played a different role, with one summoning senators to the Doge's Palace and another, the execution bell, literally sounding the death knell.

Below: grand exterior of the Basilica.

the interior appears huge, cavernous and daunting, but when your eyes have grown accustomed to the dim, mysterious light, it becomes exotic and entrancing. The mosaics cover some 4,000 sq m (43,000 sq ft) of floor, domes, arches and walls. The *pavimento* is like an oriental carpet, embellished with naturalistic and religious motifs, its undulations proving how movable the foundations of the church are. From the outside **Loggia dei Cavalli** you have a grandstand view of the Piazza and Piazzetta, just as doges and dignitaries did during processions and celebrations.

Back at ground level you are likely to be herded around the Basilica far too speedily to appreciate its treasures.

Don't miss the first two domes in the nave for some of the finest of the mosaics: the **Pentecost Dome**, which shows the Descent of the Holy Ghost as a dove, and the **Ascension Dome**, featuring Christ surrounded by Apostles, angels and the Virgin Mary.

The Altarpiece and Other Treasures
The greatest of many treasures is the **Pala d'Oro**, a superb medieval screen behind the altar. First commissioned for Doge Pietro Orseolo in the 9th century, and increasingly enriched over the years, it is encrusted with pearls, sapphires, emeralds and enamels. Even after Napoleon's looting, there are still about 2,000 jewels left.

More Byzantine loot is stored in the

Treasury (entered from the right transept). The prize piece here is the Pyx, an embossed silver-gilt casket in the shape of a Byzantine church. There are many other beautiful features in the Basilica, among them the **Baptistery** and **Zen Chapel** (both usually closed), the chapels and the rood-screen.

THE CAMPANILE

The well-restored **Campanile ❷** (Bell Tower; tel: 041-522 4064; daily July–Sept 9am–9pm, Apr–June and Oct–Nov 9am–7pm, Dec–Mar 9.30am–3.45pm; closed 3 weeks in Jan for maintenance; charge) looks much as it did when it assumed its present form in the early 16th century. This would not be surprising were it not for the fact that it collapsed in a heap on 14 July 1902. Amazingly, the only casualties were the custodian's cat and, at the foot of the tower, Sansovino's Loggetta, which was reassembled from the debris. The campanile was rebuilt exactly 'dov'era e com'era' ('where it was and how it was'). A lift takes you to the top for stunning views of the city and lagoon, and stretching on a clear day to the peaks of the Dolomites; oddly, the canals are not visible. The plaque by the exit marks the water level on 4 November 1966 – about 0.9m (3ft) above ground level.

CORRER MUSEUM

Opposite the Basilica, on the Piazza's far side, the **Museo Correr ❸** (Piazza San Marco; tel: 041-427 30892; www.muse-iciviciveneziani.it; daily Apr–Oct 9am–7pm, Nov–Mar 9am–5pm; charge) occupies some 70 rooms of the Procuratie Nuove (Offices of the Former Procurators of St Mark's) and the Ala Napoleonica (Napoleonic Wing). The museum is refreshingly free of crowds and full of historical and artistic treasures. Some grasp of Venetian history helps, though there are useful information sheets in English in each room. Particularly interesting are the sections devoted to the institution of the doge, to Venetian trade and the Arsenale. A highlight is the *Bucintoro*, the ship used to transport the doge during special processions (room 45).

Venetian Art

Art-lovers should concentrate on the **Quadreria**, a gallery of fine Venetian paintings from the 13th to the 16th centuries, including a whole room of works by the Bellinis (room 36) and the famous Carpaccio painting *Two Venetian Noblewomen* (room 38), formerly called *The Courtesans*. The ladies look bored as they wait for their husbands to return from a hunting trip – prior to research the generous cleavages led to the mistaken identity. Also worth seeking out is the detailed wood engraving of Venice carved by Jacopo de' Barbari in 1500 (room 32).

The museum also gives access, via rooms 18 and 19, to the **Museo Archeologico** (Archaeology Museum), full of Greek and Roman statuary. A highlight is the 1st-century BC Grimani Altar (room 6), with Bacchic decoration and a sensual relief of lovers in an embrace.

Above from far left: The Torre dell' Orologio also tells the sign of the zodiac; the colonnades of the Palazzo Ducale; winged lion on the Basilica facade.

Museum Pass

A museum pass (tel: 041-427 30892, www.visitmuve.it) covering the Palazzo Ducale, Correr Museum and all other civic museums, is currently available for €20.50 and valid for six months. A museum card for the museums of Piazza San Marco (Palazzo Ducale, Museo Correr, Biblioteca Marciana, Museo Archeologico) costs €15 and is valid for three months. To avoid the long queues, buy your tickets at the Correr Museum, which is rarely crowded. You can then enter the Palazzo Ducale without lining up again for a ticket.

Lions of Venice

The leonine symbol of Venice is everywhere. Pacific, playful or warlike, lions pose on flags unfurled over Grand Canal palaces, curl up in mosaics, fly as ensigns above ships, or crouch as statues in secret gardens. A golden winged Lion of St Mark still adorns the city standard and remains the symbol of the Veneto.

Below: manuscript, Biblioteca Marciana.

MARCIANA LIBRARY

Also accessible from the Museo Correr is the **Biblioteca Marciana ❹** (Marciana Library, also known as the Libreria Sansoviana; tel: 041-240 7223; www.museicivicivenezian i.it; daily Apr–Oct 9am–7pm, Nov–Mar 9am–5pm; charge), whose main hall (Sala Monumentale) has a magnificent ceiling with allegorical scenes painted by artists such as Tintoretto and Veronese. The library building, which you can admire from the Piazzetta *(see p.34)* was built by Sansovino in 1530 to house the doge's precious collection of Greek and Latin manuscripts. Palladio described it as 'the richest building since antiquity'.

Sansovino was also responsible for the severe-looking **Zecca**, where Venice minted gold and silver ducats until the fall of the Republic. The mint and treasury functioned until 1870 but is now part of the Marciana Library, with the courtyard covered over and used as a reading room.

LUNCH BREAK

It is probably time for lunch and a rest from sightseeing. Everything around the Piazza is criminally overpriced. If you're happy to splurge, enjoy the stunning views from the rooftop terrace of the **Hotel Danieli** *(see p. 111)*; if you prefer an affordable trattoria patronised by Venetians, try **Alla Rivetta**, see ⑪②, or **All'Aciugheta**, see ⑪③, both behind the Riva degli Schiavoni.

PALAZZO DUCALE

From the 9th century to the fall of the Republic in 1797, the **Palazzo Ducale ❺** (Doge's Palace; Piazza San Marco; tel: 041-427 30892; www.museicivicivenezian i.it; daily Apr–Oct 8.30am–7pm, Nov–Mar 8.30am–5.30pm; charge) was the powerhouse of Venice. It was the residence of the doges, seat of the government and venue of the law courts and prisons. By the 14th century the Venetian head of state was little more than a figurehead, or 'a glorified slave of the Republic', as Petrarch put it. But as far as living quarters went, the doge couldn't complain. No other residence could rival it,

and for many years this was the only building in Venice entitled to the name *palazzo*. Other grand residences had to be satisfied with the appellation Ca', short for *casa* (house).

The ceremonial entrance, on the Piazzetta, was the **Porta della Carta**, a magnificent piece of flamboyant Gothic architecture, showing Doge Foscari kneeling before the Lion of St Mark. Today this is the public exit, the entrance being the **Porta del Frumento** on the waterfront. From this side you can admire the shimmering pink facade, the delicate arches and the florid Gothic detail.

Palace Interior

Located near the entrance, the **Museo dell'Opera** (Works Museum) houses some of the original richly carved capitals from the palace. From here you go into the main courtyard, whose **Scala dei Giganti** (Giants' Staircase) formerly made an appropriately grandiose entry to the palace.

Inside the palace the great chambers were the meeting place for the highest levels of political and administrative systems. Huge rooms are decorated with heavily encrusted ceilings and monumental canvases, all in glorification of the great Venetian Republic. Leading artists of the day, including Tintoretto and Veronese, were commissioned to convey the idea that Venice was not just a place of power, but also one of overwhelming beauty.

The sumptuous **Scala d'Oro** (Golden Staircase) leads up to the doge's private apartments, then up again to the grand

Council Chambers. The most impressive among these are the **Anticollegio**, the waiting room for ambassadors, with Veronese's *Rape of Europe* and works by Tintoretto; the **Sala del Collegio**, with magnificent ceiling paintings by Veronese; and the **Sala del Senato**, with another elaborate ceiling, painted by Tintoretto and assistants. It was in the **Sala del Consiglio dei Dieci** that the notoriously powerful Council of 10 (in fact about 30) tried crimes against the state. Secret denunciations were posted in the *bocca di leone* (lion's mouth) in the waiting room.

After the armoury, you go back to the second floor, along Liagò Gallery, to the grandest room of all: the **Sala del Maggior Consiglio**. This was the Assembly Hall, where doges were elected and where the last doge abdicated. The proportions are monumental – some 3,000 guests were accommodated when

Food and Drink

② ALLA RIVETTA

Castello 4625, Ponte San Provolo; tel: 041-528 7302; Tue–Sun; €€

Set by the bridge across the Rio del Vin, linking Campo Santi Filippo e Giacomo and Campo San Provolo, this is an unpretentious, un-touristy place close to San Marco. Fish and seafood predominate (grills and cuttlefish), as do polenta and plates of roast vegetables. Trade is brisk, the atmosphere breezy and the service brusquely Venetian.

③ ALL'ACIUGHETA

Castello 4357, Campo Santi Filippo e Giacomo; tel: 041-522 4292; daily; €€

No longer a traditional *bacaro* (Venetian wine bar), this is still an unpretentious, if updated, inn which goes against type by having space, a terrace and a proper menu, including *polpette* (meatballs), plenty of seafood and even a selection of decent pizzas. It's popular with Venetians, tempted by the fine Friuli wines, Adriatic fish, oysters and cheeses.

Above from left:
the Piazzetta;
gondolas moored
by the waterfront.

Henry III of France was entertained here at a state banquet in 1574. The ceiling consists of panels painted by famous contemporary artists, among them Tintoretto and Veronese, whose dynamic *Apotheosis of Venice* stands out for its dramatic perspective. Tintoretto's huge *Paradise*, which covers the entire east wall, was for a long time the largest painting in the world: a staggering feat for a man of 70. Below the ceiling a frieze features the first 76 doges. Note the blacked-out space that should depict Marin Falier, the doge executed for treason in 1355.

Bridge of Sighs

From the splendour of the council rooms you are plunged, as were the prisoners, into the dungeons. The *pozzi*, the dungeons beneath the palace, were dark, dank and infested with rats; the *piombi*, where Casanova entertained and masterminded his daring escape, were salubrious in comparison. The new prisons, those you see today, are reached via the renovated **Ponte dei Sospiri** ❻ (Bridge of Sighs) – named after the sighs of prisoners as they took a last look at freedom before torture or execution. Or so the story goes. In fact, by the time the bridge was built in the 17th century, the cells were quite civilised by European standards, and used only to house petty offenders. Only one political prisoner ever crossed the bridge.

The Secret Itinerary

The 'Secret Itinerary' is a fascinating tour, in English, French or Italian, of the hidden parts of the palace, such as the torture chamber and dungeons (tours in English daily Sept–June 9.55am, 10.45am and 11.35am; booking essential, tel: 041-240 7238, or at the Palazzo Ducale information desk).

THE PIAZZETTA

Bounded by the mint, the Basilica and the Doge's Palace is the Piazzetta (Little Square) overlooking the waterfront. The quayside known as Bacino San Marco, is where foreign dignitaries and ambassadors would moor their boats as they entered the city – now there is a lively gondola stand. Pop into **Al Todaro**, see ⑪④, for a quick coffee among the gondoliers, and observe the enormous granite columns of **San Marco and San Teodoro**, brought from Constantinople in the 12th century. One column is topped by a statue of St Theodore, who was the original patron saint of the city before St Mark's remains were brought to Venice from Alexandria. The

Below: statue of
Adam on the Palazzo
Ducale, with the
Bridge of Sighs in
the background.

other column is surmounted by what appears to be a winged lion, the traditional symbol for St Mark. It is now believed this lion is actually a chimera, brought back from China; the Venetians simply added wings and transformed it into the lion of St Mark.

TORRE DELL' OROLOGIO

To the west of Piazza San Marco is the **Bacino Orseolo**, the main gondola depot, too busy a spot for a romantic ride but ideal for watching water traffic. The basin backs onto the **Procuratie Vecchie**, the earliest of the Procurators' offices.

At the far end of the building, over the archway, stands the Renaissance **Torre dell' Orologio** ❼ (Clock Tower; tel: 041-427 30892; www. museicivicivenetiani. it; guided tours in English Mon–Wed at 10am, 11am, Thur–Sun at 2pm and 3pm; reserve ahead; charge). It has a large gilt-and-blue enamel clock face, which displays the signs of the zodiac and phases of the moon. It also, of course, tells the time, with two bronze figures of Moors striking the bell on the hour. Behind the Clock Tower, shoppers can plunge into the dark alleys of the **Mercerie**. Or flee the crowds to collapse in the waterfront café **Ombra del Leone**, see ⑪⑤.

Gondola Rides

The Bacino Orseolo is the most central place to begin a gondola ride. Don't pay more than the official rate (evening trips are extra), and agree a route before setting off. For romance, stick to the back canals rather than the Grand Canal, and book a tour with the Gondoliera, the only female gondolier. Avoid the singing gondolier convoys.

Below: Caffè Florian.

VAPORETTO DOWN
THE GRAND CANAL

*The Grand Canal sweeps majestically through the heart of the city, lined
by a rich and varied parade of palaces and teeming with boats of all
descriptions. You can see it all from a vaporetto (waterbus) on this tour.*

Above: Ca d'Oro;
vaporetto No. 1.

Waterbus Pass

To take this trip slowly,
pick up a good-value
city transport pass:
€50 for 7 days, €35
for 3 days, €30 for 2
days, €20 for 24
hours; €18 for 12
hours; €7 for an hour's
journey – discount if
booked on www.
veniceconnected.com.
Validate by holding the
card up to the sensor
by the boarding pier.
Pick up a water
transport map (€3)
from the tourist office,
or Hello Venezia offices
(tel. 041-24 24, www.
hellovenezia.com).

DISTANCE 4km (2½ miles)

TIME 40 mins on vaporetto
No. 1 (30 mins on No. 2)

START Piazzale Roma vaporetto

END San Zaccaria-Danieli
vaporetto

POINTS TO NOTE

This ride is loveliest around sunset,
when the light hits the buildings and
most of the day-trippers have
departed, leaving you with a much less
crowded ride. The faster No. 2 covers
the same journey, but only makes
seven stops en route. This delightful
experience is not an alternative to
splashing out on a gondola and, time
permitting, is worth doing once again
at night, focusing on the atmospheric
palazzi on the other bank.

The Grand Canal, Venice's fabulous
highway, is nearly 4km (2½ miles) long.
The surprisingly shallow waterway is
spanned by four bridges and lined by
10 churches and more than 200 palaces.
It sweeps through six city districts
(sestieri), providing changing vistas of
palaces and warehouses, markets and
merchant clubs, courts, prisons and even
the city casino. You can see it all from

vaporetto No. 1, the waterbus that takes
it slowly, stopping at every landing stage.

The route starts from **Piazzale
Roma ❶**, in the north of Venice. You
could, of course, do it the other way
round, starting from San Marco, but this
way you have the grand finale of the
Santa Maria della Salute church and the
San Marco waterfront. Ideally do both,
giving yourself more time to absorb the
visual feast. You could start at the railway
station (Stazione Ferroviaria), but you
are guaranteed the best views from a seat
at the open-air front of the boat; for this,
you need to be one of the first to
embark, at Piazzale Roma.

PIAZZALE ROMA AND
THE STATION

As you ride towards the station, you'll
have a good view of the **Ponte Calatrava** – Venice's newest bridge, unveiled
in 2008. It was designed by acclaimed
Spanish architect Santiago Calatrava
and connects Piazzale Roma with the
railway station. A minimalist structure
of steel, glass and stone, the sinuous,
fish-tailed bridge continues to court
controversy, especially for its lack of
wheelchair access, and for its inexpli-
cably huge maintenance costs.

Venice's **Stazione Ferroviaria Santa Lucia ❷** comes into view on your left. This striking modern building was built in 1954, with its stairway offering visitors their first taste of the Venetian lagoon. Beside the station, the Baroque church of the **Scalzi** was named after the 'barefooted' *(scalzi)* Carmelite friars who founded it in the 17th century. In 1915 an Austrian bomb hit the roof, which was decorated with a fresco by Tiepolo. Fragments of the work are now in the Accademia. The vaporetto passes under the **Ponte degli Scalzi**, built in 1934 to replace a 19th-century iron structure.

FONDACO DEI TURCHI TO THE PESCHERIA

Opposite the San Marcuola stop the **Fondaco dei Turchi ❸** was a stunning Veneto-Byzantine construction before it was heavily restored in the 19th century. The former warehouse was leased to Turkish merchants; today it is home to the Museum of Natural History. Just past the landing stage on the left, the vast **Palazzo Vendramin-Calergi ❹** is one of the canal's finest Renaissance palaces, designed by Mauro Coducci. Wagner died here in 1883. Today, it is home to the city's casino.

Beyond the Baroque church of San Stae on your right looms the vast **Ca' Pesaro ❺**, designed by the only great Venetian Baroque architect, Baldassare Longhena. It houses the **Gallery of Modern Art** and **Oriental Museum** (Thur–Tue 10am–6pm; charge). Beyond it the white Ca' Corner della Regina was the birthplace of Caterina Cornaro, queen of Cyprus, in 1454.

The vaporetto recrosses the canal to the **Ca' d'Oro ❻** landing stage, by the palace of the same name. This is a landmark building, a sumptuous version of a Venetian palace. The pink-and-white filigree facade, with carved capitals, crowning pinnacles and bas-reliefs, was once covered in gold leaf – hence the name, House of Gold. The original owner, Marino Contarini, demolished a pre-existing

Above from far left: the meandering Grand Canal; cooling off on a hot day.

Chance Your Luck
To admire the Palazzo Vendramin-Calergi from afar, leave the boat at San Stae. To gamble in the impressive casino, get off at San Marcuola. It is open all year round 3pm–2am. Dress smartly and bring your passport. Wagner's mezzanine apartments here can also be visited.

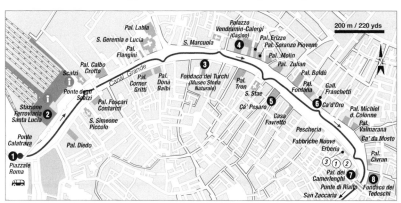

Look out for
Alilaguna's eco-
friendly Energia boats,
which cruise up and
down the Grand
Canal, connecting the
airport with the Rialto.
These airport boats
are now equipped
with electric engines,
so you won't be able
to hear them.

palace to construct this magnificent building in the early 15th century, as a demonstration of his wealth and status. The Gothic palace houses the **Galleria Franchetti**, one of the city's most appealing art galleries *(see p.78)*.

Erberia and Pescheria

Look across the canal to the **Erberia**, an introduction to the central market, where vegetables, fruit and flowers have been sold for centuries. Barges from the island of Sant' Erasmo arrive early in the morning to offload crates

of lagoon artichokes and asparagus. The newish Rialto Mercato vaporetto leads to both the bustling market and the café-lined waterfront, now one of the most sought-after spots for sunset cocktails and *cicchetti* or for embarking on a bar crawl.

Next door, fresh fish is laid out on ice under the colonnades of the mock-Gothic **Pescheria** (fish market). If you have a pass and are able to hop on and off the vaporetto at your leisure, the Erberia holds many options for eating on the canal, see 1, 2 and 3.

Food and Drink 🍴

① IL MURO

San Polo 222, Campo Bella Vienna (labelled Campo Battisti on maps); tel: 041-241 2339; www.murovinocucina.it; Mon–Sat; €–€€

Il Muro makes a a friendly stop for superb sparkling wine, cocktails and *cicchetti* (cheap but inventive tapas), or for a full meal, with outdoor tables perched right by the Rialto market. Try the *antipasto misto* (seafood sampler) or the tapas of tiny artichokes, baby meatballs, or fried mozzarella balls.

② NARANZARIA

San Polo 130, Erberia; tel: 041-724 1035; www.naranzaria.it; Tue–Sun; €€

This stylishly contemporary *osteria-enoteca* occupies a former citrus fruit warehouse. Grab an outdoor table on the Erberia for views of the Grand Canal. Besides fresh seafood carpaccio and fusion dishes, such as monkfish with saffron, or olives with fennel salad, the chef Akira serves a rare treat in Venice – sushi.

③ AL BANCOGIRO

San Polo 122, Erberia/Campo San Giacometto; tel: 041-523 2061; www.osteriabancogiro.it; Tue–Sun; €–€€

A few doors down from Naranzaria and fitting snugly into ancient Rialto porticoes, this double-aspect wine bar and new-wave *bacaro* stands on the site of the city's earliest bank. Eat *cicchetti* with locals or select from the creative but ever-changing menu upstairs, with dishes including *baccalà*, seafood risotto or calamari with lagoon artichokes. All three spots make a perfect beginning to any Rialto bar crawl, but avoid Monday when the fish market is closed.

AROUND THE RIALTO

Gondolas and traffic congestion are likely to slow you down at the **Rialto**, giving you time to take in the bridge and surrounding buildings. Just before the bridge on the right the **Palazzo dei Camerlenghi ❼** (1528) was formerly the office of the city treasurers *(camerlenghi)*. Later, it served as the state prison. Opposite, the **Fondaco dei Tedeschi ❽**, named after the German merchants who leased the emporium, and conducted a healthy trade in precious metals from German mines, this was the most important trading centre in the Rialto area. Controversially sold to Benetton, this landmark building is slated to become a shopping centre but the radical nature of architect Rem Koolhaas' designs has sent the project back to the drawing-board. Originally the facade was adorned with frescoes by Giorgione and Titian; fortunately, remaining fragments are safe in the Galleria Franchetti in the Ca' d'Oro.

RIALTO BRIDGE TO CA' FOSCARI

Next you pass the **Ponte di Rialto** (Rialto Bridge; *see p.73)*, constructed in 1588–91 after two of the previous wooden bridges had collapsed. Michelangelo, Palladio and Sansovino were among the eminent contenders for the commission for the new stone structure, but in the end the project went to the aptly named Antonio da Ponte.

Before the San Silvestro stop, on the left, are the arcaded palaces of **Ca' Loredan** and **Ca' Farsetti**, both now occupied by the mayor and city council. Beyond, the large, austere-looking **Palazzo Grimani** ❾ is a Renaissance masterpiece by Michele Sanmicheli, and now serves as the Court of Appeal.

Just before the Sant'Angelo stop, note the Renaissance **Palazzo Corner-Spinelli** ❿ (1490–1510), designed by Mauro Coducci and distinguished by its arched windows and rusticated ground floor. This became a prototype for many other *palazzi* in Venice.

Stopping at San Tomà gives you time to look across to **Palazzo Mocenigo** ⓫. Byron lived here for two years, renting the *palazzo* for £200 a year. His affair with his housekeeper ('of considerable beauty and energy… but wild as a witch and fierce as a demon') ended with the brandishing of knives and his lover hurling herself into the Grand Canal. Right on La Volta (the bend of the canal), recognisable by its distinctive pinnacles, **Palazzo Balbi** ⓬ was the chosen site for Napoleon to watch the regatta of 1807, held in his honour.

On the same side, across the tributary (Rio Foscari) the **Ca' Foscari** ⓭ was described by the art critic John Ruskin as 'the noblest example in Venice of 15th-century Gothic'. Now restored, the palace was built in 1437 for Doge Francesco Foscari; today it is the most prestigious university building.

CA' REZZONICO TO THE ACCADEMIA

The next stop is **Ca' Rezzonico** ⓮, named after what is arguably the finest Baroque palace in Venice. Designed in 1667 by Baldassare Longhena, it was at one time owned by Robert Browning's reprobate son, Pen. It was while Robert Browning was staying here that he died of bronchitis. Now the **Museo del Settecento Veneziano** (Museum of 18th-century Venice; Wed–Mon 10am–6pm; charge), it has a suitably grandiose

Above from far left: fresh fish at the Pescheria; the controversial new Ponte della Constituzione (Constitution Bridge), inaugurated in 2008; on the Rialto Bridge.

Above: Ca' Foscari; gondola on the Grand Canal.

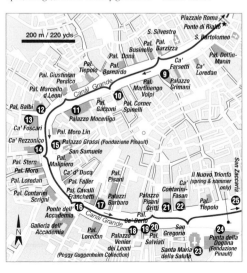

Laws of the Water

Before the 19th century, the only way to cross the Grand Canal (other than the Rialto Bridge) was on a *traghetto*, a gondola used for ferrying passengers from bank to bank. The service still criss-crosses the Canal at seven strategic points – and costs only 50 cents. Venetians normally stand, but feel free to sit. The Canal has a strict speed limit of 7kmh (4mph) – but motor boats and taxis rarely respect it. No craft apart from gondolas, or public or commercial transport, is allowed on the Grand Canal before 6pm.

rococo interior, decorated with massive chandeliers, frescoed ceilings and lacquered furniture. The second floor is a gallery of 18th-century Venetian paintings, while the third is home to the **Egidio Martini Picture Gallery**, an eclectic collection spanning five centuries. In terms of Venetian art, Ca' Rezzonico takes up where the Accademia *(see below and p.42)* leaves off.

Palazzo Grassi and the Accademia

Opposite Ca' Rezzonico is the **Palazzo Grassi** ⓫, a fine example of an 18th-century patrician residence, bought in 2005 by the French business magnate François Pinault to house his huge collection of modern art *(see below)*.

The wooden **Ponte dell'Accademia** ⓰ (Accademia Bridge) was built as a temporary structure in the 1930s to replace a heavy iron bridge. However, the Venetians were so pleased with it that it was retained. Beside the bridge on the right is the **Accademia Gallery** *(see p.42)* – the world's greatest collection of Venetian paintings, housed in a former monastery.

PALAZZO BARBARO TO SAN ZACCARIA

Beyond the bridge, the second and third adjoining buildings on the left are the Gothic **Palazzi Barbaro** ⓱. The second was a haunt of writers and artists, when the palace belonged to the Bostonian Curtis family. Among the guests were Robert Browning, John Singer Sargent, Monet, Whistler, and Henry James who wrote *The Aspern Papers* here and used it as a setting for *The Wings of a Dove*. The film of the book was also shot in the palace.

Peggy Guggenheim Collection and Palazzo Dario

On the right, the **Palazzo Venier dei Leoni** ⓲ or Palazzo Nonfinito (Unfinished Palace) is a modern-looking

François Pinault

Close to the Accademia, you may notice a strange sight. In front of a classic 18th-century *palazzo* looms a piece of contemporary art, such as a large metallic dog by Jeff Koons or a skull made of kitchen utensils by Indian artist Subodh Gupta. This is the brainchild of François Pinault, the French billionaire owner of Gucci, Chateau-Latour and Christie's auction house, who snapped up the Palazzo Grassi and unveiled it as a hub of contemporary art (Campo San Samuele, tel: 041-523 1680; for tickets tel: +39 0445 230 313 from abroad; www.palazzograssi.it; Wed–Mon 10am–7pm). Pinault's private collection holds 2,500 works, which are shown in rotation, linked to exhibitions at his latest acquisition, the Punta della Dogana *(see opposite and p.58)*. Redesigned by Tadao Ando, the ravishing gallery has helped turn this stretch of Dorsoduro into the so-called 'art mile', running down to the Guggenheim.

building, which now houses the **Peggy Guggenheim Collection** *(see p.59)*.

Two blocks on, the palace with the coloured marble and distinctive chimneys is the charming but reputedly cursed **Palazzo Ca' Dario ⑲**, built for a Venetian diplomat. Over the centuries there has been a history of murder, bankruptcy and suicide here. The last victim was industrialist Raul Gardini, owner of the palace from 1985, who shot himself during the corruption investigations of 1993.

Palazzo Salviati

Directly after Palazzo Dario, you'll note **Palazzo Salviati ⑳**, one of the newer *palazzi* on the Grand Canal. Built in 1924, this palace was the home of a well-established glass-blowing family. They took advantage of their prime real estate to do a little advertising for themselves on the facade: the prominent mosaic is completely out of place with the Renaissance-style architecture.

Palazzo Pisani-Gritti

Beyond the Santa Maria del Giglio landing stage on the left, the **Palazzo Pisani-Gritti ㉑** belonged to Doge Andrea Gritti in the 16th century. The palace became a hotel between the wars and has a roll-call of illustrious visitors. Soon after the Gritti, the tiny but exquisite **Ca' Contarini-Fasan ㉒** is known as the House of Desdemona.

Grand Finale

Standing guard at the canal entrance is the all-pervading **Santa Maria della Salute ㉓** *(see p.58)*, Longhena's Baroque masterpiece with a huge, exuberant facade, scrolls and statues and a massive dome. On the tip of the promontory, the figure of *Fortuna* on a golden globe adorns the top of the **Punta della Dogana ㉔**, the former customs house, currently home to François Pinault's fabulous contemporary art collection *(see box opposite)*.

Stay on the boat until the landing stage at **San Zaccaria ㉕** to enjoy the stunning view of the San Marco waterfront, as well as the island of San Giorgio, before disembarking.

Above from far left: the canalside and Palazzo Barbaro, near the Ponte dell'Accademia; opening night at the new Punta della Dogana contemporary art gallery.

Below: looking towards Santa Maria della Salute.

THE ACCADEMIA

This treasury of Venetian art ranges from Renaissance masterpieces and Byzantine panels to vibrant ceremonial paintings, but it is as memorable for its revealing snapshots of everyday life as for its sumptuous showpieces.

TIME 2–3 hours
START/END Entrance to the Accademia
POINTS TO NOTE
The paintings are dependent on natural light, so choose a bright morning and arrive early. Otherwise, aim for late afternoon to avoid crowds. You may find rooms closed for restoration, paintings repositioned, and others out on loan, but it remains a glorious window on Venetian art. Pace yourself, as much of the finest art is towards the end. Ideally combine a gallery visit with a walk around Dorsoduro *(Tour 7)*.

Accademia Bridge
The distinctive wooden Ponte dell'Accademia is a popular meeting place for Venetians. It is a fine spot for watching water traffic and offers great views of the Grand Canal and church of La Salute.

Colour and Light
Vibrant colour, luminosity and a supreme decorative sense distinguish the work of Venetian masters. Of the Venetian school, art critic Bernard Berenson says, 'Their colouring not only gives direct pleasure to the eye but acts like music upon the moods.'

Food and Drink 🍴
① CAFFÉ BELLE ARTI
Dorsoduro 1051A, Campo della Carità; tel: 041-277 0461; daily; €
This friendly café has outdoor tables and is a nice stop for a coffee before a trip to the Accademia. Far better for lunch is Fiore *(see p.48)*.

The collection of the **Accademia** (Campo della Carità; tel: 041-520 0345; www.gallerieaccademia.org; pre-book online; Mon 8.15am–2pm, Tue–Sun 8.15am–7.15pm; charge) is housed in Santa Maria della Carità, a complex of church, convent, cloisters and charitable confraternity. The church was deconsecrated in Napoleonic times and became a repository of work created during the Venetian Republic.

On show is the world's finest collection of Venetian paintings, with works by Mantegna, Bellini, Giorgione, Carpaccio, Titian, Tintoretto, Veronese, Tiepolo, Guardi and Canaletto. The art is mostly arranged in chronological order, dating from the 14th to 18th centuries. As the gallery is undergoing a leisurely refurbishment, the collection is in a state of flux so a rehang cannot be ruled out, particularly given the expansion plans. But the Sala Grande, the magnificent confraternity hall, can be seen in all its glory. The museum does not yet have a café but refreshments are on hand at the **Caffè Belle Arti**, see 🍴①, beside the entrance.

BYZANTINE STYLE

Room I shows the heavy influence of the Byzantine on the earliest Venetian painters. The principal exponent in

Venice was Paolo Veneziano, whose *Coronation of the Virgin*, a polyptych (panel painting) has an extravagant use of gold. Just before the steps up to Room II *(see below)*, look at the detailed rendering of figures in Michele Giambono's *Coronation of the Virgin* – a fine example of International Gothic style.

VENETIAN RENAISSANCE

Room II–V are dominated by Bellini, his school, and the early Venetian Renaissance, even if Canova's models for Titian's tomb are currently in **Room V**. Renaissance painting came late to Venice, chiefly introduced by Andrea Mantegna. Bellini was his brother-in-law and he influenced Venetian painters of successive generations, many of whom trained in his workshop. **Room II** contains one of the outstanding altarpieces of the period: Bellini's *Madonna Enthroned with Saints*.

Bellini Family

Giovanni Bellini ('Giambellino') is considered the founder of the Venetian school. His contributed expressiveness, conveying moods of grace, tenderness and poignancy. Bellini broke away from the traditional polyptych and brought the Virgin and saints together in a single natural composition called the *sacra conversazione* (sacred conversation). This painting heavily influenced Carpaccio's *Presentation of Jesus in the Temple* and Marco Basaiti's *Agony in the Garden*, both hanging in the same room.

'Giambellino' was the greatest of the Venetian Madonna painters. Along

with his father, Gentile, and brother, Jacopo, he commanded a large workshop that churned out these devotional paintings. His *Madonna and Child with St Catherine and St Mary Magdalene* demonstrates his masterly balance of grace, realism and harmony. On the opposite wall, Mantegna's *St George* typifies the dry rationality of the artist's *quattrocento* style.

Room V should also display masterpieces by Giovanni Bellini, including the lovely *Madonna of the Little Trees* and *Madonna and Child with John the Baptist and a Saint*. His evocative *Pietà* makes striking use of landscape.

Titian, Veronese and Tintoretto

Rooms VI–VIII pave the way for the High Renaissance works of art, intro-

Above from far left: the Accademia also hosts temporary exhibitions; detail of the gallery exterior.

Reflections of Glory
The Republic set great store by the State painter, with artists of the calibre of Bellini, Titian and Tintoretto expected to capture Venetian glory with vibrant depictions of ceremonial events, such as the receiving of prelates, ambassadors and dignitaries.

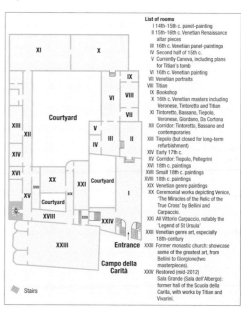

List of rooms

- I 14th–15th c. panel-painting
- II 15th–16th c. Venetian Renaissance altar pieces
- III 16th c. Venetian panel-paintings
- IV Second half of 15th c.
- V Currently Canova, including plans for Titian's tomb
- VI 16th c. Venetian painting
- VII Venetian portraits
- VIII Titian
- IX Bookshop
- X 16th c. Venetian masters including Veronese, Tintoretto and Titian
- XI Tintoretto, Bassano, Tiepolo, Veronese, Giordano, Da Cortona
- XII Corridor: Tintoretto, Bassano and contemporaries
- XIII Tiepolo (but closed for long-term refurbishment)
- XIV Early 17th c.
- XV Corridor: Tiepolo, Pellegrini
- XVI 18th c. paintings
- XVII Small 18th c. paintings
- XVIII 18th c. paintings
- XIX Venetian genre paintings
- XX Ceremonial works depicting Venice, 'The Miracles of the Relic of the True Cross' by Bellini and Carpaccio.
- XXI All Vittorio Carpaccio, notably the 'Legend of St Ursula'.
- XXII Venetian genre art, especially 18th-century
- XXIII Former monastic church: showcase some of the greatest art, from Bellini to Giorgione(two masterpieces).
- XXIV Restored (mid-2012) Sala Grande (Sala dell'Albergo): former hall of the Scuola della Carita, with works by Titian and Vivarini.

Stairs

Campo della Carità

Entrance

Below: Tiepolo's *Rape of Europa*.

ducing Titian, Tintoretto and Veronese. Titian boldly presents *St John the Baptist* as a muscular athlete in a theatrical pose. After the death of Giorgione (1510), Titian (*c.*1487–1576) dominated Venetian painting throughout his long life. Brilliant use of colour and lyrical composition are the hallmarks of his genius, on display in Room VIII. (**Room VII** currently focuses on portraits but this might change).

Typical of the first half of the 16th century are the richly coloured, exuberant paintings such as the *Sacra Conversazione* by Palma Il Vecchio in **Room VIII**. On an entirely different note is the melancholic yet penetrating *Portrait of a Young Man* by Lorenzo Lotto in the adjoining room. Acute observation of personality is a notable feature of Venetian Renaissance portraiture.

Take the steps up to **Room X** for the masterpieces of the High Renaissance, even if some are being restored. Paolo Caliari (1528–88), better known as

Veronese, as he was from Verona, painted with verve and realism. Covering one entire wall is his grandiose *Feast in the House of Levi*. It depicted *The Last Supper* but its hedonistic content (including dogs, drunkards and dwarfs) brought Veronese before the Inquisition. Rather than eliminate the offending details, however, the painter merely changed the title of the work.

Tintoretto (1518–94) was born in Venice and never moved from her shores. A man of fervent faith, he brought a kind of frenetic Mannerism to the Renaissance. His reputation was made with the striking *St Mark Rescuing the Slave*. Inspired use of shadow, foreshortening, depth and movement are typified in the dramatic *Stealing of the Body of St Mark* and *St Mark Saving a Saracen from Shipwreck*.

In the same room, Titian's dark and poignant *Pietà*, bathed in mystic light, was the artist's last gasp, painted when he was over 90 years old, possibly for his own tomb in the Frari. Veronese's *Marriage of St Catherine* and *Madonna Enthroned with Saints* are radiant, richly coloured works demonstrating his use of dazzling hues.

Tiepolo

At the far end of **Room XI** you can't miss Tiepolo's grandiose tondo, *Discovery of the True Cross*, showing his mastery of illusionistic perspective.

Room XII is currently dedicated to Tintoretto and Bassano but, when refurbished, this section of the gallery should also feature light-hearted,

lyrical, almost sugary landscapes. In the 18th century the key note in art was to delight and please the senses. Good examples are the graceful, airy *Rape of Europa* and *Apollo and Marsyas* by Tiepolo (**Room XVI**).

VIEWS OF VENICE

Topographical painting, as illustrated in **Room XVII**, was a fashion Canaletto transformed into an industry. *Perspective* is a good example of his precisely drawn scenes. Contrast Guardi's spontaneous, vibrant views of Venice. For an intimate insight into Venetian daily life in the 18th century take a look at Pietro Longhi's witty genre paintings towards the end of the room.

CEREMONIAL ART

Room XX takes you back in time to one of the highlights of the gallery: eight large canvases by five 'ceremonial artists' of the late 15th and early 16th centuries, commissioned by the Scuole Grande di San Giovanni Evangelista. The scenes, depicting the *Stories of the True Cross*, are studded with historical detail, documenting Venetian life in the 15th century. Worth singling out are Gentile Bellini's *Corpus Domini Procession*, showing Piazza San Marco and (opposite) *The Curing of a Man Possessed by Demons* by Carpaccio, showing the old wooden Rialto Bridge, which collapsed in 1524.

Room XXI is devoted to Carpaccio's intimate yet wonderfully graphic *Scenes from the Life of St Ursula*.

GIORGIONE AND BELLINI

Room XXIII, in the former monastic church, showcases masterpieces by Bellini and Giorgione, including *The Tempest*, a high point of the Venetian Renaissance. Little is known about the artist, who died of the plague when very young, but he is ranked as one of the founders of modern painting. Giorgione, who trained under Bellini, was an innovator in that he achieved his effect through the use of colour and light as opposed to line and drawing. *The Tempest* is one of his few certain attributions, but the subject still remains a mystery. Beside it, *The Old Woman*, by the same artist, is a striking piece of early realism.

The **Sala Grande (XXIV)**, the restored last room, is a work of art in itself. Also known as the Sala dell'Albergo, the former confraternity hall has a coffered ceiling and a telling triptych by Antonio Vivarini and Giovanni d'Alemagna, which charts the transition from International Gothic to Renaissance. Titian's *Presentation of the Virgin*, still occupying its original position on the entrance wall of the gallery, makes a fitting finale.

Once you've had your fill of art, satisfy your hunger at **Taverna San Trovaso**, see ⓘ⓶.

Above: detail of Veronese's *Feast in the House of Levi* (1573).

Mystical Works
The Accademia is the natural place to appreciate Bellini's mystical work before moving onto the city churches. These paintings are not all limpid, idealised Madonnas: in his poignant *Pietà*, the suffering Virgin cradles her son, her careworn face a testament to the painter's expressive powers.

Note that many of the religious works in the Accademia, by Bellini and others, come from churches that were demolished or suppressed during Napoleon's occupation of Venice.

Food and Drink

② RISTORANTE SAN TROVASO
Dorsoduro 967, Fondamenta Priuli; tel: 041-520 3703; Fri–Wed; €€
This traditional Dorsoduro eatery serves reliable seafood, as well as meat dishes. To reach it from the Accademia, follow Rio Terà Carità south and turn right onto Calle Larga Nani.

THE *SESTIERE*
OF SAN MARCO

The loop in the Grand Canal occupied by San Marco is known as 'the seven campi between the bridges', a succession of theatrical spaces, each with inviting bars and monumental palaces – and some monumental crowds.

DISTANCE 3km (2 miles)
TIME 2–3 hours
START/END Piazza San Marco
POINTS TO NOTE

This walk makes a nice add-on to Piazza San Marco (see walk 1). Once you get beyond Campo San Moisè, the crowds lighten considerably.

There's more to the *sestiere* of San Marco than its showpiece Piazza. The district is home to imposing churches, the legendary Fenice theatre and the parade of *palazzi* that flank the southern curve of the Grand Canal. This itinerary also explores some of the hidden quarters of San Marco, unknown to the hordes that cling like limpets to the central Piazza.

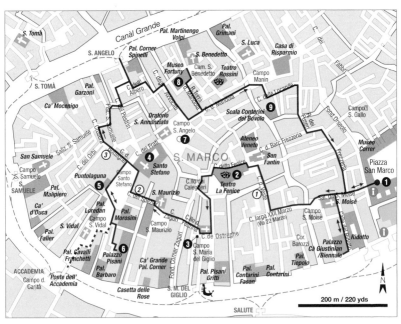

Leave **Piazza San Marco ❶** at the western end, under the arch all the way to the left. Salizzada San Moisè (where shop fronts of designers such as Louis Vuitton and Gucci may well catch your eye) leads to the church of **San Moisè**. The Baroque detail on the facade contrasts with the stark Bauer Hotel, conspicuous as one of the city's rare modern intrusions. Cross the bridge to the Calle Larga XXII Marzo, a broad up-market shopping street whose name refers to the day (22 March) when patriots reclaimed the Republic from the Austrians during the 1848 uprising.

AROUND LA FENICE

Campo San Fantin

Divert right along Calle della Veste (marked Calle del Sartor da Veste), over the bridge and into Campo San Fantin. If you're ready for a Venetian lunch on the run, consider stopping in **Vino Vino**, see ❶①, right before you enter the Campo. To your right is the Late Renaissance church of San Fantin, to the left the rebuilt **Teatro La Fenice ❷** (Campo San Fantin; reserve guided tours at the ticket office or tel: 041-2424; charge). One of the world's loveliest opera auditoriums, it was almost completely destroyed by fire in 1838, but rose again 'like a phoenix' *(fenice)*. Fire struck again in 1996. This time restorers were running up large debts for failing to complete the work on time, and two electricians were sentenced for arson, even if conspiracy theorists are unconvinced. After eight years of rebuilding, the theatre was

restored to its former glory, with every detail faithfully reproduced by Venetian craftsmen. The reopening in 2004 was celebrated with a gala performance of Verdi's *La Traviata*.

Bordering the north of the square the **Ateneo Veneto** was once the headquarters of the Scuola di San Girolamo, a charitable body whose members chaperoned criminals to the scaffold and ensured that they were given a decent burial.

Campo Santa Maria del Giglio

Take Calle de la Fenice on the right side of the theatre, go left under the colonnade and cross the bridge. Turn left into little Campiello dei Calegheri, over the bridge and along the Fondamenta della Fenice, where you can see the water entrance to the opera house. The first right turning leads you into **Campo Santa Maria del Giglio ❸**, whose church of the same name (Mon–Sat 10am–5pm; Chorus Church, *see p.100*; charge; book on www.chorusvenezia. org), with its Baroque ornamentation and secular statuary, appalled the art historian John Ruskin. The church is full of paintings, including Rubens' *Madonna with Child and St John* (in the chapel on the right).

Above from far left: inside La Fenice, one of Italy's best-known opera houses; statue of Venetian military leader Antonio Barbaro on the facade of Santa Maria del Giglio church.

Harry's Bar
Harry's Bar on Calle Vallaresso is famous for creating the Bellini, a classic cocktail of puréed peach and sparkling prosecco. Over the decades this legendary, pricey but resolutely un-glitzy watering hole has lured prominent personalities from Churchill and Charlie Chaplin to Bogart and Bacall, Fellini, Frank Sinatra and Madonna.

Food and Drink
① VINO VINO
San Marco 2007/A, Ponte delle Veste; tel: 041-241 7688; daily; cash only; €€
Charming annexe to the Antico Martini restaurant, this cosy inn serves fine wines by the glass, and hearty Venetian tapas, ranging from *sarde in saor* to *risotto di pesce* (fish). Brusque service and smiles mostly reserved for Venetian clients are the only downside.

Above from left:
Sunday morning on Campo Santo Stefano; the exquisite Scala Contarini del Bovolo.

Christmas Fair
For the past decade Campo Santo Stefano has been home to a traditional Christmas fair that attracts the local community. If you are in town during December, stop by for musical performances and booths selling regional culinary specialities and crafts.

CAMPO SANTO STEFANO

Turn right out of the square, cross over two bridges and through Campo San Maurizio, following the yellow sign for the Accademia. You will come to the large, attractively rambling **Campo Santo Stefano**. Enjoy the bustle from one of the open-air cafés, such as **Le Café**, see ②. Bull-baiting took place in the square until the early 19th century, when several spectators were killed by a falling stand. The fine Gothic church, **Santo Stefano** ❹ (Mon–Sat 10am–5pm, Sun 1–5pm; charge for sacristy), has a splendid ship's-keel roof and an inconspicuous (and normally empty) sacristy packed with dark paintings by Tintoretto and other Venetian masters.

On the western side of the **Campo Puntolaguna** ❺ is a worthy multimedia centre (tel: 041-529 3582; www.salve.it; Mon–Fri 2.30–5.30pm), which presents the case in favour of the MOSE mobile barrier. Here you can book boat tours to see the impressive environmental and engineering works designed to save Venice and the lagoon, including MOSE itself.

Off the southern end of the Campo, the massive **Palazzo Pisani** ❻ houses the Conservatory of Music, where melodious strains often waft from open windows. Just beyond the Campo San Vidal make a brief detour to the **Accademia Bridge** to admire the views of the Salute church and the Grand Canal.

Return to Campo Santo Stefano and take the slim Calle delle Botteghe opposite the church, past shops, galleries and authentic inns such as **Fiore**, see ③.

CAMPO SANT'ANGELO

Turn right down the Ramo di Piscina for the Piscina San Samuele. Take the steps up and cross two bridges for the Corte de l'Albero and access to the Grand Canal. The quayside here by the Sant' Angelo landing stage affords fine views of the *palazzi* opposite.

Back at Corte del' Albero, take the narrow street on the far side of the square, cross the bridge and turn right down Calle dei Avocati for **Campo Sant'Angelo** ❼, a noble quarter lined with palaces, where Casanova *(see opposite)* played his practical jokes. From here you can't fail to notice the alarming tilt of Santo Stefano's campanile.

MUSEO FORTUNY

Turn left into Calle Spezier (marked Rialto). A diversion marked to the left leads to the Late Gothic Palazzo For-

---

Food and Drink

② **LE CAFÉ**
San Marco 2797, Campo Santo Stefano; tel: 041-523 7201; daily; €€€€
This café serves delicious cakes, as well as *panini* and *tramezzini*. It is a good spot for sipping an alfresco spritz before dinner, while enjoying the bustle on the Campo. In colder months, Le Café also offers a selection of teas and hot chocolate.

③ **FIORE**
San Marco 3461, Calle de le Botteghe; tel: 041-523 5310; Wed–Mon; €€
Not to be confused with the pricey Da Fiore *(see p.120)*, this cosy trattoria is good value considering its chic setting. It is divided into a *bacaro* with a wide array of *cicchetti*, and a small restaurant that specialises in seasonal Venetian cuisine.

tuny, former home of Mariano Fortuny. The Catalan artist, sculptor and set designer spent much of his life in this palace. The pleated Fortuny silk dresses for which he is famed became the rage in the early 20th century. The renovated palace houses the **Museo Fortuny** ❽ (Campo San Bento 3958; tel: 041-520 0995; www.museiciviciveneziani.it; Wed–Mon 10am–6pm; charge) that displays Fortuny's atelier and fabrics, as well changing displays devoted to design, costumes or contemporary art.

CAMPO MANIN

Returning to the main Rialto route, you come to **Campo Manin**, a bleak square overlooked by the starkly modern Cassa di Risparmio. Daniele Manin, who led the Venetian uprising against the Austrians in 1848, stands with his back to the bank, looking towards the house he lived in when the rebellion was plotted.

Scala Contarini

Take the tiny street right off the Campo, signposted to the **Scala Contarini del Bovolo** ❾ (Calle delle Locande 4299; closed for restoration, www.scalabovolo. org), a jewel of a stairway that spirals up the Palazzo Contarini del Bovolo. (*Bovolo* in Venetian dialect means snail shell.) Worth a detour, even during restoration; the best bit is the exterior.

BACK TO SAN MARCO

Turn right along Calle delle Locande and right again into Calle dei Fuseri to the **Frezzeria**, the busiest shopping street in Venice. Named after the arrow makers who had workshops here, it was notorious for prostitutes, but is now home to an array of superior crafts and tourist tat. A left turn takes you back via the Salizzada San Moisè to Calle del Ridotto, and a prosecco at the Ombra del Leone *(see p.35)*.

Above: the Museo Fortuny (top and centre); the Scala Contarini del Bovolo.

Casanova's Venice

His name may be synonymous with seduction, but Casanova (1725–98) should not be dismissed as an amorous rogue. He was an adventurer, gambler, soldier, spy, musician and man of letters, who led a dissolute life entirely in keeping with the decadence of his age. In 1755, he was arrested on charges of freemasonry and licentiousness,

but managed a daring escape from the notorious Doge's Palace prisons. He then led a clandestine existence until returning to Venice in 1774, acting as a spy for the Venetian Inquisition. Casanova's Venice is still largely intact: you can see his birthplace in the romantic San Samuele quarter, or visit Campo Sant'Angelo, where he indulged in childish pranks, untying moored gondolas or summoning sleeping midwives and priests to imaginary emergencies. From his home, the city's finest clubs and salons were within easy walking distance, including gambling dens in the Frezzeria such as the Ridotto, the casino where Casanova learnt his trade.

QUIET CORNERS OF CASTELLO

Castello is a mix of sophistication and sleepy charm. Beyond the bustle of Riva degli Schiavoni, the district offers a slice of everyday life, where dark alleys open into bright squares, flanked by some of the city's finest churches.

Above: canal near San Lorenzo; the Campanile from the Riva degli Schiavoni.

Libertine Nuns

It is hard to associate the peaceful Campo San Zaccaria with its sinister reputation for skulduggery and licence. Three doges were assassinated in the vicinity, while the adjoining Benedictine convent was a byword for lascivious living. Since noblewomen were often despatched to nunneries to save money on dowries, tales of libertine nuns were rife.

DISTANCE 1.5km (1 mile)
TIME 2–3 hours
START Molo
END Santi Giovanni e Paolo
POINTS TO NOTE
This walk can easily be combined with walk 11 (done in reverse) via a short walk to Santa Maria dei Miracoli.

Lying to the north and east of San Marco, this *sestiere* is the largest in Venice, and warrants two separate walks. This one explores the western side of the district and covers some of the finest art and architectural treasures in the city. Starting at the bustling waterfront close to San Marco, you work your way north through quiet streets and squares to the great Gothic church of Santi Giovanni e Paolo (San Zanipolo). This walk is the perfect antidote to monumental Venice and the grandeur of San Marco.

THE MOLO

Start at the **Molo ❶**, the busy waterfront to the south of the Doge's Palace, where gondolas sway by the quayside and camera-clicking crowds

admire the views across the water to the shimmering island of San Giorgio Maggiore. Pick your way through stalls of souvenirs and cross the Ponte della Paglia. Look left for the **Ponte dei Sospiri** (Bridge of Sighs; *see p.34*).

Riva degli Schiavoni

Now cross a bridge to the mercantile **Riva degli Schiavoni**, a long, curving promenade skirting the *sestiere* of Castello, and named after the Dalmatian sailors who used to moor their boats and barges along the waterfront. It is still a scene of intense activity, as vaporetti, *motoscafi*, barges, tugs and cruisers moor at the landing stages, and ferries chug across to the islands. The Riva is lined with distinguished hotels, the most historic of which is the **Hotel Danieli** *(see p.32 and 111)*. Favoured by the likes of Wagner, Dickens, Proust and Balzac, it still attracts the rich and famous.

SAN ZACCARIA

Cross the colonnaded Ponte del Vin and take the second turning to the left, under the *sottoportego* (covered passageway) signposted to San Zaccaria. This brings you to a quiet *campo*, flanked on one side by the part-Gothic

and part-Renaissance facade of the church of **San Zaccaria ❷** (Mon–Sat 10am–noon, 4–6pm, Sun 4–6pm; charge). The upper section, by leading Renaissance architect Mauro Coducci, has been well restored. In the 16th century the adjoining convent – not unlike other convents in the city – was notorious for its riotous, amoral nuns.

Inside the church, start with the chapels and (often flooded) crypt, reached by an entrance on the right-hand side. If closed, apply to the custodian. The Chapel of St Athanasius, with paintings by Palma Vecchio, Titian and Tintoretto, leads to the Capella di San Tarasio, the former chancel. The Vivarini family executed the glorious altarpieces, with their ornate gilded frames, which are a fine example of the Gothic painting style that was in fashion before the Renaissance took hold in Venice.

The greatest work of art – Giovanni Bellini's glorious *Sacra Conversazione* – is in the main church, above the first altarpiece on the left. This is one of the most beguiling paintings in Venice. Here, Bellini created a new type of religious painting, not based on a story from the Bible, but rather a scene where serene, meditative figures gather for a 'sacred conversation', embraced by soft shadow and rich, mellow hues.

SAN GIORGIO DEGLI SCHIAVONI

Leave the church and the square via the archway. Turn right into Campo San Provolo, go under the *sottoportego* and

you will come into the charming quayside of **Fondamenta dell'Osmarin**. On a corner on the far side of the canal is the red-brick Palazzo Priuli, a fine Venetian Gothic palace. At the end of the canal cross the two bridges and look right to the Greek Orthodox church of **San Giorgio dei Greci** distinguished by its dome and tall, tilting bell tower. Take the narrow alley straight ahead, pass Campiello della Fraterna on the left, and join Salizzada dei Greci. The

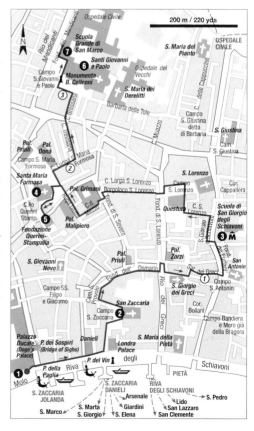

Meet La Gondoliera

Gondoliera Alex Hai, famous as 'the first female gondolier', has risen above prejudice from male peers to create her own vision of the gondolier's role. Devoid of the classic spiel and showmanship of macho Venetian boatmen, she prefers to weave a spell while rowing you through the beguiling backwaters. Whether painting an historical portrait of Venice or recounting her ghostly experiences, she evokes a sense of the underbelly of the city. Especially on a night tour, it is hard not to be won over by tales of palaces floating, slipping and sliding, or simply to revel in the companionable silence as you skirt the back canals.
(To book Alex, tel: +39 348 302 9067, primagondoliera@gmail.com.)

Trattoria da Remigio, see ⑪①, is a good option for an authentic lunch if the mood strikes.

At the far end of the street cross over the bridge and turn left. Follow the canal along the Fondamenta dei Furlani for the **Scuola di San Giorgio degli Schiavoni ❸** (Calle dei Furiani 3259A; tel: 041-5228828; Mon 2.45-6pm, Tue–Sat 9.15am–1pm, 2.45–6pm, Sun 9.15am–1pm; variable slightly reduced hours in low season; charge), founded by the Slavs from Dalmatia to protect their community in Venice. The tiny Scuola is decorated with an exquisite frieze of paintings by Carpaccio illustrating the lives of the Dalmatian patron saints, St George, St Tryphon and St Jerome. The scenes are rich in colour, remarkably vivid and detailed, giving a good idea of life in Venice in the early 16th century. This delightful spot makes a perfect companion to the Accademia *(see 42)*, which also showcases Venice's most endearing painter.

SANTA MARIA FORMOSA

Coming out of the Scuola, cross the bridge and turn right, following the canal northwards. Shortly before a portico take a left turn down the Calle San Lorenzo for the church of **San Lorenzo**, now a hospice. Marco Polo is said to have been buried here, but his tomb was lost when the church was rebuilt in 1592. Cross the bridge at the other side of the square, turn immediately right, then first left down the Borgoloco San Lorenzo. Cross the canal of San Severo, pausing on the bridge to see some fine *palazzi*, pass under the dark and narrow *sottoportego*, carry straight on, then take a right turn for the lovely **Campo di Santa Maria Formosa**. This charming, rambling square, once the site of bullfights and masked balls, is full of Venetian life, with market stalls and open-air cafés. It is flanked by *palazzi* and dominated by the swelling apses of Coducci's church of **Santa Maria Formosa ❹** (Mon–Sat 10am–5pm, Sun 1–5pm; charge). Don't miss Palma il Vecchio's polyptych of *St Barbara and Saints*, adorning the chapel of the Scuola dei Bombardieri. The same artist painted portraits of Francesco and Paolo Querini, who built the 16th-century Querini-Stampalia palace south of the square. Today the building houses the **Fondazione Querini-Stampalia ❺** (Tue–Sun 10am–6pm, Fri–Sat until 10pm; charge), comprising a delightful little gallery of Venetian paintings, a library, garden, café, and a splendid room where concerts of Baroque music are staged.

If ready for lunch in this most Venetian of squares, take in the backchat between the market traders and gondoliers before moving on. Resist the *campo*'s cheerful pizzerias in favour of a more memorable meal. Just around the corner lies the convivial **Al Mascaròn**, see ⑪②, tucked away in Calle Lunga Santa Maria Formosa, the narrow street east of the square.

Take the tiny street almost opposite Al Mascaròn, cross the quiet canal and go straight on for Campo Santi Giovanni e Paolo.

CAMPO SAN ZANIPOLO

The church of **Santi Giovanni e Paolo** ❻ (daily 7.30am–12.30pm, 3.30–7.30pm; charge) is better known as San Zanipolo. This huge brick edifice vies with the Frari as the city's greatest Gothic church. After the tiny streets of Castello its towering form makes a dramatic impact. Known as the Pantheon of Venice, it contains the tombs of 25 doges. Identifying them is only possible with a detailed guide or the official booklet, available in the sacristy. Finest of all is Tullio Lombardo's *Monument to Doge Andrea Vendramin* (1476–8), on the left side of the apse. Paintings to single out are Giovanni Bellini's *St Vin-cent Ferrer* polyptych, over the second altar on the right, and the Veronese ceiling paintings in the Rosary Chapel.

Scuola Grande di San Marco
The unadorned facade of Zanipolo is flanked by the ornate **Scuola Grande di San Marco** ❼, once the meeting house of silk-dealers and goldsmiths, now the civic hospital (ambulances are usually moored in the adjoining canal). Look for the *trompe l'oeil* arches framing lions that appear to be looking from the far end of deep Renaissance porticos – in fact they are barely 15cm (6in) deep. At the end of your walk, relax in the **Antico Caffè Rosa Salva**, see ⑪③.

Above from far left: washing day in Castello; stained glass in San Zanipolo.

Monument to a Mercenary Close to the *scuola* stands one of the finest Renaissance equestrian statues, a monument to a vainglorious mercenary *(condottiere)* Bartolomeo Colleoni, by Verrocchio.

Below left: *St Barbara and Saints* by Palma Il Vecchio, detail, Santa Maria Formosa church.

Food and Drink 🍴

① TRATTORIA DA REMIGIO
Castello 3416, Salizzada dei Greci; tel: 041-523 0089; Wed–Mon am; €€
This timeless trattoria, a local favourite, is immune to trends. Set in a revitalised area, it offers an authentic Venetian mood and a menu featuring meat, cuttlefish and grilled fish, with gnocchi a house speciality. Service is friendly but can be slow. Book in advance.

② AL MASCARÒN
Castello 5225, Calle Lunga Santa Maria Formosa; tel: 041-522 5995; Mon–Sat; €€
Although no longer a secret, and no longer cheap, this homely yet arty *osteria* is still friendly and dependable, with hearty, straightforward dishes ranging from Adriatic fish to the freshest *antipasti*, bean soup and mixed grills; save room for the delicious Burano biscuits dipped in dessert wine.

③ ANTICO CAFFÈ ROSA SALVA
Castello 6779, Campo Santi Giovanni e Paolo; tel: 041-522 7949; daily; €
This is the hub of a famous *pasticceria* that has been around since 1879. You can snack on sandwiches or toasties or indulge in delicious pastries. Better yet, treat yourself to one of their home-made *gelato* sundaes, such as the 'Coppa Golosa' (ice cream, fruit salad, whipped cream and strawberry syrup).

THE EASTERN REACHES OF CASTELLO

This leisurely stroll takes you through eastern Castello, a workaday quarter far removed from the madding crowds of San Marco, taking in a variety of lesser-known sights.

DISTANCE 2.5km (1½ miles)
TIME 2 hours
START Arsenale landing stage
END Giardini landing stage
POINTS TO NOTE

Between the Arsenale, Museo Storico Navale and Giardini Pubblici, this walk is great for families. You can arrive at the Arsenale landing via vaporetti Nos 1 and 2.

For Children

If travelling with children, the Biennale gardens present a good opportunity to enjoy a little greenery and open space. The gardens have a small playground with swings and games, including ping-pong tables (though you must supply your own paddles and balls).

As this area is rarely crowded, except during the Biennale, this walk is perfect for those looking to escape the masses. It begins with the Arsenale, where the great Venetian galleys were built, goes on to San Pietro di Castello, the former cathedral of Venice, and ends in the Giardini Pubblici, home to the Biennale contemporary art extravaganza.

Food and Drink

① **EL REFOLO**
Castello 1580, Via Garibaldi; no tel; daily in summer, closed Mon in winter; €
This *enoteca* is tiny, but what it lacks in space, it makes up for in warmth. Expect unusual wines and imaginative sandwiches made with wild boar mortadella or Alpine cheeses, as well as *bigoli in salsa* (buckwheat pasta in an anchovy and onion sauce). The bar's hardcore clientele hug the bar or spill out onto Via Garibaldi.

THE ARSENALE

From the **Arsenale landing stage ❶** east of San Marco turn right (as you face inland), cross the bridge and turn immediately left. Stop on the wooden bridge over the Rio dell'Arsenale for the best views of the entrance to the **Arsenale ❷**, the old Venetian shipyard that became the symbol of Venetian maritime might *(see box on p.56)*. Heralding the shipyard is the great Renaissance gateway, guarded by stone lions plundered from Piraeus, the great shipyard in Athens, Greece. Beside the triumphal arch is a relief of Dante and a plaque recording his reference to the Arsenale in *The Divine Comedy*. The writer came here in 1306 and 1321, and the scene of frenzied activity left a lasting impression.

Naval History Museum

Back on the main waterfront stands the dignified **Museo Storico Navale ❸** (Campo San Biagio; tel: 041-520 0276; Mon–Fri 8.45am–1.30pm, Sat 8.45am–1pm; charge). Given the tantalising elusiveness of the Arsenale, the Naval History Museum is the only place where you can fully appreciate the greatness of maritime Venice. Before its

present incarnation, the 16th-century building was used as a naval granary and biscuit warehouse. Models of Venetian craft include the original gondolas, complete with *félze* or cabin (the 'shelter of sweet sins'), and a replica of the lavish *Bucintoro*, the doge's state barge.

AROUND VIA GARIBALDI

Beyond the next bridge turn inland for the **Via Garibaldi ❹**. The widest street in Venice, it was created by Napoleon in 1808 by filling in the canal here. The street is lined with basic grocery shops, food stalls and friendly bars and restaurants. If you're looking to grab a glass of wine, try the small **El Refolo**, see ⑨①, where clients spill out onto the street. On the right you soon come to the unkempt end of the **Giardini Pubblici** (Public Gardens) fronted by a bronze monument to the revolutionary leader Garibaldi. Keep straight ahead for the

Rio di Sant'Anna, where you will find a colourful barge selling vegetables – one of the last surviving floating markets in the city. Take the first turning on the left (marked Calle San Gioachino). A little bridge crosses a canal festooned with laundry and flanked by brightly coloured boats. Cross a bridge into Calle Riello and then turn left for Campo di Ruga, and beyond the square on Salizada Stretta take the second turning on the right and cross the bridge for the island of San Pietro.

THE ISLAND OF SAN PIETRO DI CASTELLO

The beautiful but seriously listing campanile in front of you was the work of Mauro Coducci in 1482–8. This is the bell tower for **San Pietro di Castello ❺** (Mon–Sat 10am–5pm; Chorus Church, *see p.100*; charge, www.chorusvenezia.org). It seems

Above from far left: the Canale di San Pietro; the Arsenale's impressive Porta Magna (main gate).

Above: Arsenale lions and canons; the Canal d'Arsenale and the gateway into the old Venetian shipyard.

Great Explorers
On Via Garibaldi, the first house on the right, marked with a plaque, was home to the Italian explorers and navigators John Cabot and his son Sebastian, who discovered the Labrador coast of Newfoundland (mistaken at the time as the coast of China) for the English crown.

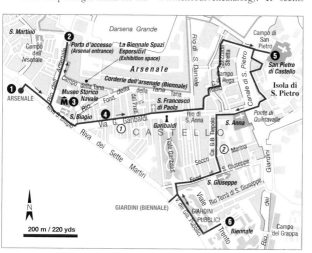

Above from left:
the tranquil cloister of San Pietro di Castello; Santa Maria della Salute *(left)*, a highlight of the Dorsoduro walk.

remarkable that this remote church, set on a grassy square, was the Venetian seat of religious power. It was built to a Palladian design in 1557 on the site of a former castle (hence 'Castello'). Until 1807, when the bishop (later patriarch) was transferred to the Basilica of San Marco, this was Venice's cathedral.

Take the path behind the Campanile and recross the Canale di San Pietro over the Ponte di Quintavalle bridge.

From here you can see boatyards and fishing smacks. Pass the crumbling ex-church and monastery, **Sant'Anna**, on your left, then take the first left into Calle G.B. Tiepolo (which from the street is marked Campiello Correra).

Carry straight on and then turn left onto Seco Marina, where you will find the favourite local eatery, **Dai Tosi**, see ①②, a good place to stop for a spot of lunch. This is a working-class neighbourhood, and you are likely to be eating with more local people than tourists.

From the Fondamenta San Giuseppe, turn right, heading south to the main waterfront and Giardini Pubblici. Boat enthusiasts will enjoy the waterfront here. Everything that floats, from gondolas, tugs and yachts to the large Lido ferries and ocean-going liners, seems to ply the waters of the inner lagoon.

Food and Drink

② DAI TOSI

Castello 738, Seco Marina; tel: 041-523 7102; Thur–Tue; €

This simple but pleasant trattoria and pizzeria comes into its own during the Biennale as the exhibition is staged in the nearby Giardini. Outside the Biennale, Dai Tosi attracts a younger crowd, drawn to the pizzas and keen to dine in the garden in summer. If you fancy something besides pizza, try the spaghetti with scampi.

In the Navy

The word *arsenale* derives from the Arabic *darsina'a*, a house of industry, an apt description of this production line. The Arsenale was a city within a city bounded by 3km (2 miles) of walls, with wet and dry docks, ordnance depots and an armaments site envied abroad. At its peak it was the greatest shipyard in the world, with 16,000 'arsenalotti' churning out galleys. The fastest time was recorded in 1574, when Henry III of France visited the city. The workers created an entire galley in the time it took him to consume a state banquet. The shipyard was destroyed by Napoleon in the 1790s, the cannons and bronzes melted down to create monuments celebrating the French Revolution. Slowly, parts of the Arsenale are being reclaimed as exhibition spaces, especially during the Biennale. These include the Corderie, the renovated ropeworks, and the 16th-century shipyards known as the Gaggiandre. As the chief workshop for the MOSE mobile dam, the Arsenale is re-enacting its ancient role – minus the fireworks, of course.

LA BIENNALE

If you are here in an odd-numbered year between June and November, join the glamorous art crowd at the **Biennale ❻**, a highlight of the international art calendar. More than 30 permanent pavilions in the gardens display contemporary art from different nations. Although for much of the rest of the time the pavilions remain empty, they are at least now used for other events such as the Biennale dell'Architettura, which is held in the intervening years between September and November.

From the Giardini landing stage you can jump onto a No. 2 vaporetto going westwards and enjoy the sublime views as you head back to San Marco.

DORSODURO

Stroll along the Zattere quayside, visit galleries in the chic eastern quarter of the Dorsoduro, then retreat to one of Venice's liveliest squares. End by going off the beaten track to visit two of the city's loveliest churches.

Dorsoduro simply means 'hard back', so called because the district occupies the largest area of firm land in Venice. It is the most attractive quarter for idle wandering, with wisteria-clad walls, secret gardens and a distinctly arty air. Apart from the Accademia and La Salute basilica, the district is surprisingly quiet, even if the creation of new art galleries along the Zattere has confirmed Dorsoduro as a hub for contemporary art. The southern spur of the Zattere makes the most enchanting Venetian promenade.

THE ZATTERE

Start at the **Zattere landing stage ❶**, which is serviced by waterbus No. 2. The Zattere, which means floating rafts, from the days when cargo was off-loaded here, is a beguiling quayside awash with art galleries, open-air cafés and canalside views. If the urge for an ice cream takes you, stop at **Nico**, see ⓘ①. From here, turn right onto the Fondamenta Nani, which offers a captivating view, across the canal, of the **Squero di San Trovaso ❷**, one of the last surviving gondola yards. The construction of a gondola is highly complex, involving 280 pieces of timber, cut from nine different types of wood. The boats constantly come in for scraping, tarring and overhauling,

> **DISTANCE** 3.5km (2¼ miles)
> **TIME** 4–5 hours
> **START** Zattere landing stage
> **END** San Basilio landing stage
> **POINTS TO NOTE**
>
> This walk can be combined with San Giorgio and the Giudecca (walk 8) by taking the No. 2 vaporetto from the Giudecca Palanca stop to the Zattere.

but, as at the other *squeri*, there are only around four new gondolas constructed here each year. The craftsmen used to come from the Dolomites, hence the Alpine look of the *squero*.

The next stop on the Zattere is the church of the **Gesuati ❸** (Mon–Sat 10am–5pm; Chorus Church, *see p.100*; charge), just east of the landing stage. The grandiose church is a supreme

Food and Drink 🍴
① NICO

Dorsoduro 922, Zattere; tel: 041-522 5293; Fri–Wed; €

Nico is the best place to buy a *gelato* to eat while strolling along the waterfront. Nico specialises in the wickedly calorific *gianduiotto* (chocolate hazelnut with whipped cream). There are a small number of tables outside if you want to eat your cool treat while enjoying the view.

Above: domestic, down-tempo Venice; pulpit detail, Angelo Raffaele, Dorsoduro.

Gondola Craftsmen

El Felze is an association of artisans who make gondolas and gondola-related items. Founded by Roberto Tramontin, owner of the Trovaso *squero*, they often organise events, and their website (www. elfelze.com) is a treasure trove of information about gondola design and production, also listing addresses for gondola yards.

Festa della Madonna

The Feast of the Salute, when a temporary wooden bridge is laid down over the Grand Canal to connect La Salute basilica with the San Marco neighbourhood, is held each year on 21 November. Venetians then traditionally cross this bridge to pay homage to the Virgin Mary and pray for good health.

example of 18th-century Venetian architecture, and holds Tiepolo masterpieces in their original setting (1739).

Further along the Zattere is **La Calcina Pensione**, otherwise known as Ruskin's House. The art historian stayed here when it was a simple inn, frequented by artists.

Follow the quayside, past the Casa degli Incurabili, a former hospice, to the **Magazzini del Sale ❹**, the Salt Warehouses that helped found 15th-century Venetian fortunes. These are now used for art exhibitions and events, as is the sister space, revamped by Renzo Piano, the **Fondazione Vedova** (tel: 041-779 5503; www.fondazion-evedova.org for both venues; Wed–Mon 10.30am–6pm; charge). Virtually next door to the latter, stop for refreshment at the arty **Linea d'Ombra**, see ⑪②.

Punta della Dogana

Commanding the point is the **Punta della Dogana ❺** (Wed–Mon 10am–7pm; charge), a cutting-edge showcase for contemporary art, belonging to French tycoon François Pinault. It forms an integral whole with the Palazzo Grassi, further down the Grand Canal *(see p.40)*, and, for conservative Venice, is a bold new step.

SANTA MARIA DELLA SALUTE

Rounding the peninsula, you come to Longhena's monumental church of **Santa Maria della Salute ❻** (Campo della Salute; 9am–noon, 3–6.30pm, until 5.30pm in winter; church free, charge for sacristy), erected to commemorate the deliverance of Venice from the plague of 1630. A Baroque

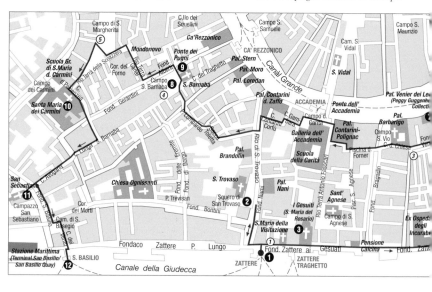

church of massive proportions, it took over half a century to build and is supported by over a million timber piles. After the exuberance of the facade, the grey-and-white interior is surprisingly severe. The highlights are the works by Tintoretto and Titian in the sacristy (often open only in the afternoon).

GUGGENHEIM

Back in Campo della Salute, cross the tiny bridge to the Campo San Gregorio, where the deconsecrated Gothic brick church of **San Gregorio** is now used as a workshop for restoring paintings. Continue to the little Campiello Barbaro, overlooked by the ill-fated Palazzo Ca' Dario *(see p.41)* and on over a bridge to the Palazzo Venier dei Leoni, housing the **Peggy Guggenheim Collection** ❼ (enter from Calle

S. Cristoforo or Fondamenta Venier dei Leoni 701; tel: 041- 240 5411; www.guggenheim-venice.it; Wed–Mon 10am–6pm; charge). Peggy Guggenheim (1898–1979), the eccentric American heiress, bought the palace in 1949 and lived here until her death.

The city's most visited gallery after the Accademia, it has a collection featuring works from almost every modern art movement of the 20th century. The majority of the works came directly from the artists, many of whom she patronised, befriended, entertained and – in the case of Max Ernst – married. Picasso, Pollock, Magritte, Mondrian, Brancusi and Giacometti are just a few of the big names. The collection is light, airy and welcoming, with well-displayed canvases, a sculpture garden and good café.

CAMPO SAN VIO

Following the route eastwards along the Fondamenta Venier dei Leoni you come to **Campo San Vio**, one of those rare Venetian squares in which you can sit on a bench and lap up the bustle on the Grand Canal. On the bridge before the square is **Ai Gondolieri**, see

Food and Drink

② **LINEA D'OMBRA**
Dorsoduro 19, Ponte dell'Umiltà, Zattere; tel: 041-2411 881; Wed–Mon; €€€
Facing the Il Redentore church on the Giudecca, this romantic restaurant and wine bar is perfect on a summer's evening, especially if you can secure a table on the pontoon. Creative cuisine and vaguely reinterpreted Venetian classics, including seabass in a crust or tuna tartare. Book in summer.

Above from left: caffè life in Dorsoduro; the Giudecca.

Floating Market
On the far side of the Ponte dei Pugni, you can see a colourful barge crammed with fresh fruit and vegetables – one of the last of Venice's floating markets.

⑪③. It's a short walk to Campo della Carità and the **Accademia** *(covered in Walk 3; see p.42)*.

WESTERN DORSODURO

From Campo della Carità, zigzag along the streets beyond the Accademia, and cross the Rio di San Trovaso at the first bridge. Follow the flow to **Campo San Barnaba ❽**, passing artisans' studios. Once home to the impoverished nobility, today the district is dominated by students who stop for an ice cream at **Grom**, ⑪④, on the square here.

Ponte dei Pugni

Exit from the north end of the square, turning left onto Fondamenta Gerardini and crossing the **Ponte dei Pugni ❾** (Bridge of Fists). The marble footprints on the bridge marked the starting spot for fist-fights between the Nicolotti, from the parish of San Nicolò, and the Castellani, from Castello. Originally

there were no railings on the bridge, and opponents would throw each other into the canal. After several fatalities the fights were banned in 1705.

The Carmini and San Sebastiano

Carry on down Rio Terrà Canal, where you will pass the mask shop, **Mondonovo**, at No. 3063. A left at the end leads into Campo di Santa Margherita, bustling with local life, and normally full of students from the nearby Ca' Foscari University. **Bar Margaret Duchamp**, see ⑪⑤, is especially good for a spritz in the sun.

At the far end of the square is the church and *scuola* of the **Carmini ❿** (Campo Carmini; church: Mon–Sat 2.30–5.30pm; free; *scuola*: daily 11am–4pm; charge). The *scuola* houses Tiepolo's sensational ceiling painting *St Simon Stock Receiving the Scapula of the Carmelite Order from the Virgin*.

From here, go right down Calle della Pazienza, cross the first bridge, then turn right onto Calle Lunga San Barnaba, leading to the church of **San Sebastiano ⓫** (Mon–Sat 10am–5pm; charge), reached across a tiny bridge. The church is a virtual museum of Paolo Veronese, its ceilings, frieze, choir, altar, organ doors and sacristy decorated with the artist's glowing and joyous works of art. This was Veronese's parish church, and, fittingly, he is buried here.

Cross the bridge out of the square and follow Fondamenta San Basilio south to the Zattere. A No. 2 vaporetto from **San Basilio ⓬** will take you back to San Marco or via the Stazione Marittima towards the north of the city.

Food and Drink 🍴

③ AI GONDOLIERI
Dorsoduro 366, Ponte del Formager; tel: 041-528 6396; Wed–Mon; €€€
Old-school formality and, unusually for Venice, a fish-free, meat-based menu, which is strong on lagoon vegetables and pasta.

④ GROM
Dorsoduro 2461, Campo San Barnaba; tel: 041-099 1751; daily; €
This purist Piedmontese ice-cream chain only uses the freshest ingredients, from Piedmontese hazelnuts to Amalfi lemons.

⑤ MARGARET DUCHAMP
Dorsoduro 3019, Campo di Santa Margherita; tel: 041-528 6255; daily; €
One of the best-known bars on the square, it is perfect for a coffee or spritz in the sun.

SAN GIORGIO MAGGIORE AND THE GIUDECCA

Enjoy vistas of familiar Venetian landmarks, as the vaporetto chugs across the Canal of San Marco to the island of San Giorgio Maggiore. Then head towards the Giudecca, taking in grand views across the Giudecca canal and fine architecture by Palladio.

San Giorgio is the closest of the lagoon islands to the city, and the only major island untouched by commerce. Seen from afar, the majestic monastery appears suspended in the inner lagoon, with its cool Palladian church matched by a bell tower modelled on that of San Marco. Together with the Baroque beacon of La Salute, these two great symbols guard the inner harbour of Venice. Giudecca, just off Dorsoduro, is also celebrated for its Palladian church, while Elton John's Gothic home is a more recent addition to the list of land-

DISTANCE 3km (2 miles)
TIME 2 hours
START San Zaccaria vaporetto
END Giudecca–Palanca vaporetto
POINTS TO NOTE
This walk is especially pleasant done from late afternoon to early evening, in order to see the sunset across the Giudecca canal. Just be sure to time it so that you will still be able to see the interiors of the churches.

Jewish Community
The name Giudecca was derived either from the community of Jews who lived here or from the word '*giudicati*' or 'judged', dating from the time when troublesome nobles were banished here.

Below: San Giorgio Maggiore boasts a spectacular setting.

marks. Locals credit the rock star with turning the tide in this old working-class district, which is undergoing a rebirth with the restoration of residential and industrial buildings.

SAN GIORGIO MAGGIORE

From the **San Zaccaria** ❶ ferry stop near San Marco, it is just a short jaunt on a No. 2 vaporetto (going clockwise) to San Giorgio Maggiore. The island was given to the Benedictines in the 10th century, and their monastery was one of the most important in the city. Seen from San Marco, the island sits stage-like in the inner lagoon, set off by its soaring campanile. The vaporetto deposits you directly in front of the church, with its Palladian facade modelled on an ancient temple.

Started by Palladio in 1566, and finished after his death in 1610, **San Giorgio Maggiore** ❷ (May–Sept Mon–Sat 9.30am–6.30pm, Sun 8.30–11am, 2.30–6.30pm, Oct–Apr until 5.30pm; church free, charge for bell tower) is cool, spacious and perfectly proportioned. It is also home to two powerful works by Tintoretto: *The Last Supper* and *Gathering of the Manna*, both executed when he was almost 80. For one of the most impressive panoramas in Venice, have a monk accompany you in a lift to the top of the tower. The view is even more spectacular than that from Piazza San Marco's across the water.

FONDAZIONE CINI

Coming out of the church, turn right out of the *campo* and follow the unmarked *fondamenta* until you reach Palladio's monastery, now the **Fondazione Cini** ❸ (tel: 041-2201215; www.cini.it; tours Sat–Sun 10am and 4pm; charge). The foundation studies Venetian civilisation, and hosts contemporary exhibitions, concerts and events. On guided tours, you can visit the cross-vaulted refectory, Longhena's library and the Palladian Cloister of the Cypresses that leads to the monastic gardens and the Teatro Verde open-air theatre, which

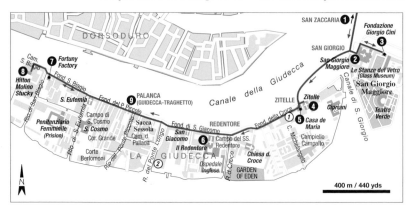

provides an atmospheric setting for occasional summer concerts.

THE GIUDECCA

Pick up a second No. 2 vaporetto heading westwards – they go about every 10 minutes. The boat makes three stops on the island on La Giudecca. This is Venice's most diverse neighbourhood: earthy working-class pockets interspersed with palatial hotels, factories converted into funky designer flats, and monasteries converted into crafts centres. At best, Giudecca feels like an authentic community, with an influx of arty incomers living cheek-by-jowl with gondola-makers, boat-repairers, sailors, celebrities and crafts-people.

The Zitelle

Disembark at the first stop, Zitelle, in front of the church of the same name. The **Zitelle ❹** (Sun at 10am for Mass only) was designed by Palladio, though completed after his death. The

adjoining buildings, which now form the Bauer Palladio hotel, originally provided shelter for young women without a dowry and taught them lacemaking. Behind the Zitelle is the luxurious Hotel Cipriani *(see p.115)*, normally accessed by private boat.

Casa de Maria

Just right of the church is the most innovative building on the Giudecca, the **Casa de Maria ❺**. Built from 1910 to 1913, this elaborate building was named after its architect, a Bolognese painter called Mario de Maria. The patterned brickwork facade is reminiscent of the Palazzo Ducale, while the three luminous windows are a modern hybrid of traditional Venetian Gothic architecture. Continue west down the Fondamenta to **I Figli delle Stelle**, see ⑪①, a welcoming lunch stop.

Favourite Colour
'Of all the colours, none is more proper for churches than white, since the purity of the colour, as of life itself, is particularly satisfying to God.'
                    Palladio

Below:
Fondazione Cini.

Food and Drink 🍴
① I FIGLI DELLE STELLE
Giudecca 70/71, Fondamenta delle Zitelle; tel: 041-523 0004; Tue–Sun lunch; €€
Sleekly decorated, and graced with a spectacular view across the Giudecca canal, this romantic restaurant combines creative cuisine with healthy dishes from Puglia, where the chef comes from. Try the *frittura di pesce e verdure*, a delicious mix of lightly battered seafood and vegetables. Reserve for outdoor seating as this is a popular spot for Venetians too.

Il Redentore

A small bridge on the Fondamenta leads to the Campo del Sanitissimo Redentore and one of Venice's most conspicuous landmarks. Palladio's **Il Redentore** ❻ (Mon–Sat 10am–5pm; Chorus Church; charge), built to commemorate the deliverance of Venice from the 1576 plague, which took 50,000 lives. This graceful church is the scene of Venice's most beguiling festival *(see box below)*. The interior, strikingly stark and solemn, is a fine example of classical rationality.

Continue westwards, maybe making a detour to Giudecca's boatyard, the Cantiere Crea, home to a gondola workshop, a marina and a new Venetian crafts centre, Arti Veneziane alla Giudecca, as well as housing the inn, **Al Storico da Crea**, see ⑪②. To get there, turn inland down the first narrow *sottoportego* after Calle San Giacomo and walk through the boatyard. The crafts centre showcases ancient skills, with master-craftsmen demonstrating mask-making and gondola-building, as well as selling Murano glass and Burano lace.

Molino Stucky

Keep heading west, crossing Ponte Longo, and looking out for the boat-lined canal and the artificial island of **Sacca Sessola** beyond. Around the Palanca waterfront lie a cluster of bars, of which **Alla Palanca** is the best.

After another bridge, you will come to No. 805, the **Fortuny Factory** ❼ (Mon–Fri 9am–12.30pm, 2–5pm), which has been producing Fortuny fabrics *(see p.18)* since 1922. Next door is the neo-Gothic **Molino Stucky** ❽, a former grain silo and flour mill converted into a luxury hotel *(see p.115)*.

From here, backtrack to the **Palanca landing** ❾ and take No. 2 vaporetto back to the main island. If you're lucky, you might make the Hilton shuttle boat, which heads towards Piazza San Marco.

Feast of the Redeemer

La Festa del Redentore, held on the third Sunday of July, is the most touching and intimate of Venetian festivals. It focuses on Il Redentore, the Palladian church built as a token of thanks after salvation from the plague of 1576. Venetians wend their way to the church carrying candles and reciting the rosary. A sweeping bridge of boats stretches across the Giudecca canal to the church, enabling people to attend Mass and listen to the chanting monks. The firework display on the eve of the feast day has been a feature since the 16th century. At night, crowds line the Zattere and the Giudecca or take to boats of every description, many decorated to create a fabulous night spectacle. Foghorns are sounded and fireworks blaze over the lagoon.

Food and Drink 🍴

② RISTORANTE AL STORICO CREA
Giudecca 212, Cantiere Nautica; tel: 041-296 0373; www.alstoricoristorante.com; €€
Perched above the busy boatyard, and founded by a champion gondolier and gondola-maker, this timeless spot serves Venetian fish, pasta and vegetable dishes along with lagoon views – and old seadog tales if you're lucky enough to catch 'Crea' himself.

SAN POLO AND SANTA CROCE

*Stroll through the quiet neighbourhoods of San Polo and Santa Croce,
a warren of alleys and homely squares that hide the great treasures of
Bellini, Titian and Tintoretto in the Frari and Scuola di San Rocco.*

San Polo and Santa Croce form adjoining districts curved into the left bank of the Grand Canal. Together they encompass the bustling Rialto market *(see p.70)* and the picturesque backwaters towards the station, centred on the quintessential *campo* of San Giacomo dell' Orio.

SCUOLA DI SAN ROCCO

This circular tour begins and ends at the **San Tomà vaporetto ❶**. Heading north from here, take the second right into the small Campo San Tomà. On the far side of the square you will see the former Scuola dei Calegheri; once the shoemakers' and cobblers' confraternity, it is now used as a public library. Follow the signs for the Scuola di San Rocco, one of the greatest city sights.

The **Scuola Grande di San Rocco ❷** (Salizzada San Rocco; tel: 041-523 4864; www.scuolagrandesanrocco.it; daily 9.30am–5.30pm; charge) is the grandest of the *scuole*, or charitable lay fraternities, and acts as a backdrop for Baroque recitals. The society is dedicated to St Roch, the French saint of plague victims, who so impressed the Venetians that they stole his relics and canonised him.

DISTANCE 2.5km (1½ miles)
TIME 3–4 hours
START/END San Tomà vaporetto
POINTS TO NOTE
As these neighbourhoods are relatively quiet, this makes a great walk for the weekend, when other people make a beeline for Piazza San Marco. It can be linked with Dorsoduro *(see walk 7)* by doing it in reverse and heading south into Campo Santa Margherita after the Scuola di San Rocco.

The 16th-century building is also a shrine to the great Mannerist painter Tintoretto. He was one of several eminent contenders for the decoration of the Scuola, Veronese among them, but caught his competitors unawares by producing a completed painting, rather than the requested cartoon. He worked on the Scuola on and off for 24 years, producing powerful biblical scenes. As you go round, note the artist's extraordinary ability to convey theatrical effect through contrasts of light and shade, bold foreshortening, visionary effects of colour and unusual viewpoints.

In the lower hall the paintings illustrate scenes from the *Life of the Virgin*,

The Scuole
The *scuole* were charitable lay associations, which looked after members' spiritual, moral and material welfare. Serving the citizen class from lawyers and merchants to skilled artisans, the *scuole* were expected to support the State and contribute to good causes. For the merchant class, excluded from government, this was an opportunity to show civic pride.

Titian

Titian (c.1487–1576), the great master of Venetian painting, was actually born on the mainland in the small town of Pieve da Cadore. He was sent to Venice at a young age to study painting and spent the rest of his life here until his death, aged 89. His greatest paintings are in the Frari.

while the upper hall has paintings over 4.8m (16ft) high, depicting scenes from the *Life of Christ* and, on the ceiling, images from the Old Testament. Use the mirrors provided to view the ceiling without straining your neck.

At the far end of the Sala dell' Albergo, scenes from *The Passion* culminate in *The Crucifixion* itself, fittingly the largest, most moving and dramatic painting of the collection. *The Glorification of St Roch* on the ceiling of the same room was the work that won Tintoretto the commission.

THE FRARI CHURCH

Retrace your steps to the Salizzada San Rocco, stopping for a pick-me-up *gelato*

at **Millevoglie**, see ⑪①. From here you can see the apse end of the **Frari Church ❸** (Campo dei Frari; Mon–Sat 10am–6pm, Sun 1–6pm; Chorus Church, *see p.100*; charge), which abuts Campo San Rocco. Follow the side of the church around, taking in its simple Gothic brick facade before entering.

Along with the church of Santi Giovanni e Paolo *(see p.53)* in Castello, the Frari is the finest Gothic church in Venice. The hulking bare-brick building and adjoining monastic cloisters were built in the 14th and 15th centuries by Franciscan friars, whose first principle was poverty – hence the meagre decoration of the facade. The soaring bell tower is the tallest in Venice, after the campanile in Piazza San Marco *(see p.31)*. It is currently being restored, after instability was detected in 2006.

The Interior

Inside, the eye is drawn to Titian's gloriously rich *Assumption of the Virgin*, which crowns the main altar. On the left side of the church the same artist's *Madonna di Ca' Pesaro* is another masterpiece of light, colour and harmony, and a very daring work that was one of the earliest to show the Madonna out of the centre of the composition. Members of the Pesaro family, who commissioned the work, can be seen in the lower half of the painting. Directly opposite is Titian's mausoleum, erected 300 years after his death.

Other outstanding works of art here include Giovanni Bellini's beautiful *Madonna and Child with Saints* in the sacristy, of which Henry James wrote,

'Nothing in Venice is more perfect than this'; the finely carved 15th-century monks' choir; the wooden statue by Donatello of St John the Baptist on the altarpiece to the right of the main altar; and the sinister monument to Canova (to the left of the side door).

SCUOLA DI SAN GIOVANNI EVANGELISTA

Back in Campo dei Frari, cross the bridge out of the square and turn left onto Fondamenta dei Frari. Cross another bridge, turn left, and then right onto Calle del Magazen and the **Scuola di San Giovanni Evangelista** ❹. The church is part of a labyrinthine quarter of narrow alleys *(calli)* and covered passageways *(sottoporteghi)*. Though the Scuola is only open by appointment (tel: 041-718 234; www. scuolasangiovanni.it), the exterior courtyard is lovely, while the theatrical interior can be seen by anyone attending an opera at the confraternity house. Established in 1261, the Scuola was one of the six major confraternities, largely due to its ownership of a piece of the True Cross, and played a leading role in the ceremonial life of the city.

Highlights

The first courtyard has a marble screen designed by Pietro Lombardo, which is watched over by an eagle, the evangelical symbol for St John, the confraternity's patron saint. The second courtyard features a relief of the members of the confraternity kneeling

before St John. The inscription below records the purchase of the land for the Scuola in 1349.

SANTA CROCE

Exiting the courtyard, turn left and stroll down the street, soaking up the local flavour in this quiet section of town. A little way along, look out for a small courtyard on the right with a terracotta pavement laid in a herringbone pattern. At one time, most of Venice's streets were paved in this fashion. At the end of the street, turn left and cross the bridge over the canal, entering into **Campiello del Cristo**.

We are now in the *sestiere* of Santa Croce. Though centrally located, this district is bypassed by the majority of tourists, probably because of its lack of 'big name' sites. But thankfully this affords the opportunity to enjoy a slice of real Venetian life. The bridge offers a nice view of an enclosed garden with large trees, evidence that many homes do have gardens, even in Venice.

Go straight through the *campiello*, continuing to Campo San Nazario Sauro. Heading east out of the square via the Ruga Bella brings you to the enchanting **Campo San Giacomo dell'Orio** ❺. Here you will find Venetians

Above: Campo San Giacomo dell' Orio; marble screen, Scuola Grande di San Giovanni Evangelista.

Food and Drink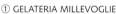

① GELATERIA MILLEVOGLIE
San Polo 3033; Salizzada San Rocco; tel: 041-524 4667; daily until late; €
Millevoglie (behind the Frari church) is reputed to be the area's best ice-cream parlour – a good enough reason to seek it out on a sweltering day. Try the fig and tiramisu flavours.

Above from left: striking Cuor di Bue tomatoes for sale; carnival masks.

Off the Beaten Track
Linger for a drink in the friendly San Polo neighbourhood. Calle della Madonetta is a pleasant alley that runs over bridges and under buildings towards the Rialto. This is one of several adjoining streets with overhanging roofs, a rarity in Venice.

young and old gathering to chat in the cafés, gossip on the red benches or shop at the small grocery. Take the time to relax, maybe join local people for a drink at **Al Prosecco**, see ⑪②, or have a meal at **Il Refolo**, see ⑪③.

PALAZZO MOCENIGO

The tour now begins to loop back to San Polo. Exit from Campo San Giacomo dell'Orio via the road that runs next to Al Prosecco. Follow the signs to the vaporetto and you will soon reach **Palazzo Mocenigo** ❻ (Salizzada San Stae 1992; tel: 041-721 798; www.museiciviciveneziani.it; Tue–Sun 10am–5pm, until 4pm in winter; charge), ancestral residence of one of the greatest dogal families and now home to an eclectic collection of period costume, ranging from corsets to knee-breeches, mainly from the

18th and 19th centuries. It is also a great chance to view a 17th-century palatial mansion, with its opulent furnishings intact, and the portrait gallery of a dynasty that produced seven doges.

CAMPO SAN POLO

Leaving the *palazzo*, take a left and continue along the street that led you here, cross over two bridges, then turn right into Campo Santa Maria Mater Domini. Cross the *campo*, taking the street as far as you can before turning left onto Rio Terà Bernardo. Following the street south will lead you directly into **Campo di San Polo** ❼, the largest square in Venice after Piazza San Marco. It has none of the grandeur of San Marco but is nonetheless beautiful in its own busy way. Once the site of bull-baiting, tournaments, masked balls and fairs, it is now the scene of less festive activities such as football and cycling. You might decide to have lunch on the square at this point, at **Antica Birreria la Corte**, see ⑪④; this is also a good late-night option, if you'd prefer to come back another time.

Highlights

The **church of San Polo** ❽ (Mon–Sat 10am–5pm; Chorus Church, *see p.100*; charge) is worth a visit for the cycle of the *Stations of the Cross* by Tiepolo (follow the sign for the Crucis del Tiepolo) and Tintoretto's *Last Supper*.

Next to the church, the classical **Palazzo Corner-Mocenigo** was for a while the residence of Frederick Rolfe (self-styled Baron Corvo), the notor-

---

Food and Drink

② AL PROSECCO
Santa Croce 1503, Campo San Giacomo dell'Orio; tel: 041-524 0 222; Mon–Sat; €€
Friendly owners Stefano and Davide run this small *enoteca*. Wines by the glass (including superior Prosecco) accompany a good selection of cheeses, *salumi* (cold cuts) and salads, all sampled in a charming neighbourhood campo.

③ IL REFOLO
Campiello del Piovan, Campo San Giacomo dell'Orio; tel: 041-524 0016; closed all day Mon and Tues lunch; €–€€
In a pretty canalside setting, this innovative, upmarket pizzeria is the place for a peaceful candlelit dinner in an out-of-the way spot.

④ ANTICA BIRRERIA LA CORTE
San Polo 2168, Campo San Polo; tel: 041-275 0570; daily; €€
This former brewery represents good value, and offers ample outdoor and indoor seating, which makes it a popular option for large groups. Inventive salads, good-value pizza, and beer, of course.

iously eccentric English writer. It was here that he wrote *The Desire and Pursuit of the Whole*, ruthlessly lampooning English society in Venice. As a result his host threw him out, penniless, onto the streets. On the opposite side of the square is the **Palazzo Soranzo** with its sweeping pink Gothic facade.

MASK SHOPS

Turn right out of the church and cross the bridge. Along **Calle dei Saoneri** and the streets beyond, sequined mask and souvenir shops have replaced some of the Venetian craft shops, but it's still fun for browsing, and the occasional artisan can be spotted creating glass insects, fashioning a traditional leather mask or making marble-effect paper. At the end of Calle dei Saoneri, turn left, then right into Calle dei Nomboli. Halfway along, the stunning masks in the window of **Tragicomica** (No.

2800, tel: 041-721 102) are handmade by craftsmen – hence the prices. Masks range from *commedia dell'arte* characters to allegorical masks of the creator's own invention, as well as *commedia dell'arte* Carnival costumes for hire or sale.

CASA GOLDONI

Opposite the shop is **Casa Goldoni** **❾** (Calle dei Nomboli 2794; tel: 041-275 9325; www.museiciviciviciveneziani.it; Thur–Tue Apr–Oct 10am–5pm, Nov–Mar 10am–4pm; charge), birthplace of the 18th-century dramatist. Carlo Goldoni's plays are known for their wit, and for his espousal of *commedia dell'arte*, creating a new genre known as *opera buffa* (comic opera). Like many of the private residences or confraternity houses on this itinerary, this place is often used for concerts and recitals. From here, follow signs for the vaporetto back to San Tomà.

Above: *Goldoni.*

Venetian Crafts
The craft tradition goes beyond masks and glass. For Carnival costumes, the finest costumier is Atelier Nicolao; the most sought-after old-fashioned printer is Gianni Basso. You could do a ceramics course at the celebrated Orsini or a bookbinding course with Paolo Olbi; or buy handbags at Malfatte (meaning misdeeds), crafted by female prisoners at Giudecca prison.

Commedia dell'Arte

Many of the most distinctive carnival masks and costumes are inspired by characters from the *commedia dell'arte*. The essentially comic genre emerged in 16th-century Italy and featured improvisation, a fast pace and witty regional parodies. The plot was often secondary to the acrobatics, juggling and miming that kept the performance lively. Stock characters based on regional stereotypes appeared in each performance, identified by their mask. Some of the most recognisable characters are: Arlecchino (Harlequin), the witty, clown-like servant from Bergamo; Pantalone, the miserly Venetian merchant; Dottore, the pompous scholar from Bologna; and Colombina, the wily and clever Venetian female counterpart to Arlecchino.

THE RIALTO

To Venetians, the Rialto is not restricted to the graceful bridge, but embraces the district curved around the middle bend of the Grand Canal – a labyrinth of dark alleys and tiny squares centred on its quayside markets.

DISTANCE 1.5km (1 mile)

TIME 2 hours

START Rialto Mercato vaporetto

END Taverna Campiello del Remer (on the opposite bank)

POINTS TO NOTE

Make an early start to see the markets in full swing and watch the barges offloading at the quayside by the Grand Canal. The best days to do this tour are Tuesday to Saturday, when both main markets are functioning.

For centuries the Rialto has been the commercial hub of the city. It was here that the first inhabitants of the lagoon are said to have settled. By the heyday of the Republic it was one of the major financial quarters of Europe – a thriving centre for bankers, brokers and merchants. The Rialto remains a hive of commercial activity. Threading through the maze of alleys is an intoxicating experience, especially in the morning. Ignore the tourist tat in favour of food-stuffs galore and sampling *cicchetti* (Venetian snacks) in one of the remaining *bacari* (traditional wine bars).

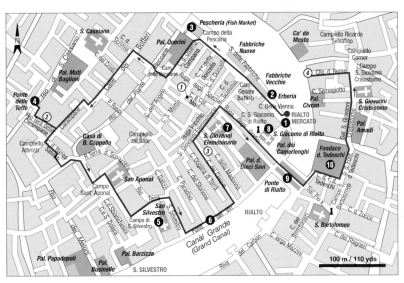

RIALTO MARKETS

Set off from the **Rialto Mercato vaporetto** and walk straight ahead into Campo Bella Vienna, a bustling square that is home to Il Muro, an inviting *bacaro, (see p.38)*.

Erberia

Turn right onto the Casaria, lined with market stalls and butchers' shops, which will deliver you into the heart of the fruit-and-vegetable market known as the **Erberia** ❷. These stalls create one of the most colourful scenes in Venice, with prized lagoon artichokes, gleaming aubergines, thick sticks of asparagus, yellow-flowered courgettes, bags of lemons and bunches of coriander. With the approach of summer come wild strawberries, plump peaches, cherries, figs and watermelons – as well as hordes of Venetians, keen to sun themselves outside the Erberia's waterfont *bacari*.

Pescheria

The market extends along the canal banks to the **Pescheria** ❸, the fish market in an arcaded neo-Gothic hall by the quayside, where gleaming sardines, sole and skate, sea bass and spider crabs, squid and live shrimps are all laid out in trays. Much of the fish and seafood is brought in from Chioggia, a fishing town situated on a small island at the southern entrance of the lagoon.

Turn left down Calle Beccarie into Campo delle Beccarie, and, if the mood takes you, join fishmongers for a prosecco and tapas at **Do Mori**, see ❶❶ or one of the other Rialto *bacari*.

BEYOND THE RIALTO

Leave the Campo via the wrought-iron bridge in the corner and follow the yellow sign for Ca' Pesaro under the *sottoportego*. Turn left onto Calle dei Botteri, ignoring the bossy yellow signs, and follow the street until it narrows, and turn right into the little square marked Carampane. Pass under the *sottoportego*, then take a right into Rio Terà delle Carampane. The first bridge on your right is the **Ponte delle Tette** ❹ (Bridge of Breasts), named after the prostitutes (there were some 11,000 in 16th-century Venice) who frequented this quarter, stripping to the waist to entice customers.

Return to the Rio Terà delle Carampane and stop for a leisurely lunch at **Antiche Carampane**, see ❶❷.

SAN SILVESTRO

After lunch, take a right onto Calle Albrizzi, then follow Calle Tamossi left

Above from far left: the Rialto Bridge; fresh fish for sale at the Rialto market.

Parmesan and Prosciutto

As you enter Campo Bella Vienna you may notice a large crowd outside the Casa del Parmigiano. This long-established shop stocks an amazing array of delectable cheeses and cured meats from all over Italy, but resist them in favour of sampling similar things at *bacari* such as Il Muro (see Tour 2, p.38).

Food and Drink

① DO MORI

San Polo 429; Calle Do Mori; tel: 041-525 401; daily; €

This ancient Rialto inn is the most picturesque of *bacari*, with its cosy atmosphere and copper pots hanging from the ceiling. Service is slightly brusque, and the prosecco not the finest, but the *cicchetti* are reliable and include *francobolli* (literally postage stamps), tiny treats of traditional tapas, from slivers of dried salt cod to tiny meatballs or sweet and sour sardines.

② ANTICHE CARAMPANE

San Polo 1911; Rio Terà delle Carampane; tel: 041-524 0165; www.antichecarampane.com; Tue–Sat; €€€

Not easy to find, but worth the search because the seafood dishes are excellent, even if service doesn't always come with a smile. You can eat at outside tables in summer.

Backstreet *Bacari*

The Rialto market marks the start of a Venetian bar crawl, a *giro di ombre*, in the backstreet wine and tapas bars known as *bacari*. Expect an array of exotic Venetian snacks *(cicchetti)* and glasses of wine *(ombre)* in snug, rough-and-ready bars, often dating back to the 15th century. Traditional Rialto bars close early so either go for lunch or for an early supper.

Below: Rialto Bridge street lamp.

until you reach a canal. Cross the bridge and follow Calle del Ponte Storto into Campo Sant'Aponal. This square may be tiny, but with eight streets leading into it, it is a crowded crossroads. The deconsecrated church of Sant'Aponal is used as an archive. Cross the Campo and head south under the *sottoportego*, into Campo di San Silvestro.

Originally founded in the 12th century, the church of **San Silvestro ❺** (daily 8–11.30am, 3.30–6.30pm; free) was completely rebuilt during the 19th century (the facade was completed in 1909). The highlight of the neo-classical interior is Tintoretto's *Baptism of Christ* (first altar on the right).

Pass in front of the church and turn right into Calle San Silvestro, which leads back to the Grand Canal. Turn

left onto the **Fondamenta del Vin ❻**, where barrels of wine used to be unloaded. It is overrun by souvenir stalls and dire touristy restaurants, but don't be drawn in by the beseeching waiters. It's a typical Venetian dilemma: the choice between lovely food or lovely waterside views, but rarely both. There are some delightful exceptions, including the *bacari* around the Erberia, but only break this rule on the Fondamenta del Vin if there's a water pageant, when a canalside view is worth an underwhelming seafood platter. For now, stroll along the canal until Sottoportego dei Cinque, where coffee connoisseurs should stop for a treat at **Caffè del Doge**, see ⑪③.

SAN GIOVANNI AND SAN GIACOMO

Continue up Calle dei Cinque, and turn right into San Giovanni Elemosinario, lined with souvenir stalls and teeming with people making their way to the Rialto Bridge. Tucked away behind a metal gate on your right, the church of **San Giovanni Elemosinario ❼** (Mon–Sat 10am–5pm; Chorus Church, *see p.100*; charge) is one of the oldest churches in the area. Pop in here to see Titian's altarpiece *San Giovanni Elemosinario*, a touching portrayal of the saint giving alms; it is characterised by the loose brush strokes that would mark the artist's later works.

Turn right outside the church, then right again onto Ruga degli Orefici, passing the oldest church in the area, **San Giacomo di Rialto ❽**. Nestling

comfortably among the fruit-and-vegetable stalls, the church is linked to St James, patron saint of goldsmiths and pilgrims. Both were much in evidence in the Rialto. Its most distinctive features are the Gothic portico, bell tower and bold 24-hour clock.

Campo San Giacomo preserves its mercantile atmosphere, an echo of Republican times, when moneychangers and bankers set up their tables under the church portico, and in the neighbouring **Bancogiro**, now a wine bar. The **Gobbo di Rialto** (Hunchback of the Rialto), is a curious stooped figure supporting the steps opposite the church: it was on the adjoining podium that republican laws were proclaimed, with the burden borne metaphorically by this figure of the Venetian Everyman.

RIALTO BRIDGE

The **Ponte di Rialto** ❾ spans the Grand Canal with a strong, elegantly curved arch of marble, a single-span bridge lined with shops. Until the 1850s, it was the only fixed point for crossing the canal. The current structure is actually the fourth version of the bridge. The first wooden structure was erected in the 14th century, only to be destroyed during a revolt in 1310. A second structure collapsed under the weight of spectators who had gathered to watch the procession for the Marquis of Ferrara in 1444. One can see what the third version looked like by viewing Carpaccio's *Miracle of the True Cross* in the Accademia *(see Tour 3, p.42)*. The current bridge was designed by the appropriately named Antonio da Ponte at the end of the 16th century. The relatively unknown architect won the commission over giants such as Michelangelo, Sansovino and Palladio. Walk along the side aisles, if possible, as they tend to be less crowded than the centre, and afford better views of the palaces, warehouses and water traffic.

THE RIGHT BANK

The building across the bridge to the left is the **Fondaco dei Tedeschi** ❿, named after the German merchants who leased the emporium *(see p.37)*. Turn left around the back of the building (away from the sign for San Marco) and cross the bridge into Campo San Giovanni Cristostomo. For a truly Venetian experience, take the alley on the left, next to the Fiaschetteria Toscana, follow the street under the *sottoportego* and you will reach the **Taverna del Campiello Remer**, see ⑪④.

Above from far left: the Grand Canal, viewed through the Rialto Bridge; strolling through the Rialto market.

Count Francesco da Mosto

Architect, writer and broadcaster Francesco da Mosto is familiar to many as a champion of Venice, both through his books and his documentaries. The count lives in Ca' da Mosto, a stately pile on the Grand Canal, and still sees the Rialto as heart and belly of his home city. *Francesco's Kitchen* (Ebury Press) combines family recipes, ancestral secrets and foodie haunts around the lagoon city.

Food and Drink

③ CAFFE DEL DOGE

San Polo 609; Calle dei Cinque; tel: 041-522 7787; Mon–Sat; €
Sniff out the best coffee in Venice at a bustling coffee house where they roast their own Arabica beans. Venetian celebrity chef Enrica Rocca also recommends the Giacometto, 'coffee blended with hazelnut chocolate, cream and toasted almonds, an orgasmic experience'.

④ TAVERNA DEL CAMPIELLO REMER

Cannaregio 5701; Campiello del Remer; tel: 041-522 5789; www.alremer.com (for useful map); Thur–Tue; €€
This hard-to-find *taverna* is deservedly popular for its romantic canalside setting, mellow mood and generous food. A stylish crowd come for the lunch-time buffet (only €20 with wine); Happy Hour with *cicchetti* (5.30–7.30pm); and live music every night, from piano to soul or jazz. Only book for the *à la carte* restaurant.

CANNAREGIO

Largely residential, Cannaregio is one of the most fascinating but least explored areas of the city. In this half-day tour you visit the world's oldest Ghetto, the peaceful backwaters of the Madonna dell'Orto neighbourhood, and some of the finest Gothic and Renaissance churches in Venice.

Above: Star of David in the Ghetto; Ca' d'Oro.

DISTANCE 3km (2 miles)
TIME 3–4 hours
START Stazione Ferroviaria
END Santa Maria dei Miracoli
POINTS TO NOTE

In summer, this walk is best done early in the morning or late in the afternoon to escape the heat. You might also want to avoid Saturdays, as it's the Sabbath, and most of the Ghetto is closed. The walk can easily be combined with walk 5 (done in reverse) via a short walk to Campo SS Giovanni e Paolo.

Cannaregio is the most densely populated district and the closest to both the railway station and the mainland. It has a neighbourhood feel, with every parish possessing its own church and *campo*. Despite post-war tenements on the fringes of the district, Cannaregio is alive with activity, chattering children and dozing cats. Glimpses of everyday life on secluded balconies or through half-shuttered blinds reveal elderly Venetians passing the time of day with their neighbours, or leaning out of windows hung with washing. The tangle of alleys reveals the occasional *bottega* selling woodcarvings, as

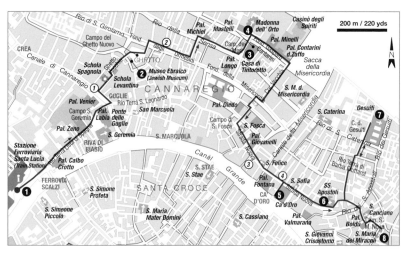

well as hole-in-the-wall bars and small *alimentari* (grocery stores), a rarity in more up-market parts of Venice.

LISTA DI SPAGNA

Start at the **Stazione Ferroviaria S. Lucia ❶** (Train Station) and follow the flow along the Lista di Spagna, then take the Ponte delle Guglie (Bridge of the Obelisks) across the Cannaregio Canal. This waterway was the main entrance to the city before the railway bridge was built in 1846 to link the city to the mainland. This is a lively quarter with waterside stalls and a morning market along the Rio Terrà San Leonardo ahead of you.

THE GHETTO

Turn left after the bridge where you see a yellow sign in Hebrew and Italian directing you to the Synagogue, and take the third covered passage on the right sign-posted 'Sinagoghe'. Before continuing, you might consider a Kosher bite to eat at **Gam-Gam**, see ⑪①.

This passageway, dotted with small shops, galleries and workshops, leads to the **Ghetto Vecchio** (Old Ghetto) and Campiello delle Scuole. Cross the bridge into the **Campo del Ghetto Nuovo** (New Ghetto Square), which, despite the name, stands at the heart of world's oldest ghetto, a fortified island created in 1516. In the early 16th century, Jews in Venice were confined to this island. It became one of the major Jewish communities in Europe with a population density three times greater

than in the most crowded Christian suburb. The only answer to these cramped conditions was to build upwards. Hence the 'skyscrapers' of Venice, tenement blocks of five or six storeys that were once the highest in Europe. The community remained on the site until 1797, when Napoleon had the gates torn down, and from then on Jews had the freedom to live wherever they liked in the city. Today, only a handful of Jewish families live here, but the area is rich in Jewish culture, with restaurants, bakeries, B&Bs and Jewish handicrafts that serve the 500-strong Jewish community in Venice.

The most striking feature of the large Campo del Ghetto Nuovo is the series of evocative bas-reliefs recording the Nazi holocaust, by Arbit Blatas. You will see them on the near side of the square, below symbolic strips of barbed wire. Three of Venice's five remaining synagogues are set around the square.

Jewish Museum

The **Museo Ebraico ❷** (Campo del Ghetto Nuovo 2902/b; tel: 041-715 359; www.museoebraico.it; Sun–Thur June–Sept 10am–7pm, Oct–May 10am–6pm, Fri until 4.30pm all year; charge) lies on the opposite side of

Art Theft
In the north aisle of Madonna dell'Orto you might notice an empty sculpted frame. This held a painting of the Madonna by Giovanni Bellini, which was stolen in 1993, and the frame has remained empty ever since.

Below:
The Ca d'Oro houses a fine collection of Renaissance art.

the square. From here English and Italian guided tours of the Spanish, German and Levantine synagogues take place from 10.30am.

Fondamenta degli Ormesini

Take the northern exit from the square, cross the bridge with wrought-iron railings and turn right into the **Fonda menta degli Ormesini**. The bustling quaysides and neighbourhood mood may also help explain why Cannaregio has such good *bacari*. With its affordable prices and picturesque canalside setting, **Al Timon**, see ⑪②, may tempt you to take a break for a glass of wine and light meal.

TINTORETTO'S NEIGHBOURHOOD

Turn left down the narrow Calle del Forno, cross the bridge and turn right into the pretty Fondamenta della Sensa. Follow the canal as far as **Campo dei Mori**. The statues here depict merchants of the Mastelli family, who came to Venice from the Peloponnese in the 12th century.

Tintoretto's House

Beyond the Campo, another turbaned merchant occupies a niche in the wall, just before the **Casa di Tintoretto ❸** (Fondamenta dei Mori 3399). The nondescript building is marked with a plaque and bas-relief of the artist, who lived here with his family from 1574 until his death in 1594. Jacopo Robusti derived his nickname, Tintoretto, from his father's profession of dyer *(tintore)*. He spent his whole life in Cannaregio and only left Venice once.

Towards Madonna dell'Orto

Return to the Campo dei Mori, cross the bridge on the far side and turn right for views of the relief of a one-legged man and a camel on the canal facade of the Gothic **Palazzo Mastelli**, which adds to the Eastern flavour of this area.

Nearby awaits the lovely **Madonna dell'Orto ❹** (Campo della Madonna dell'Orto; Mon–Sat 10am–5pm; Chorus Church, *see p.100*; charge), a masterpiece of Venetian Gothic, conspicuous for its oriental campanile, richly embellished facade and beautiful carved portal. Inside it showcases

Tintoretto's paintings, arguably his finest outside the Scuola di San Rocco *(see p.65)*. This was the artist's beloved parish church, and he is buried in the chapel to the right of the altar.

Wander around this quiet neighbourhood, where window boxes are bright with flowers, washing flaps in the breeze and cats doze in sunlit squares. This is one of the few areas of Venice where gardens are a feature.

CA' D'ORO

Follow the canal eastwards, crossing the bridge at the end. From here you can catch glimpses across the lagoon of the islands of San Michele *(see below)* and Murano *(see p.79)*. Continue to the end of the street, crossing over three bridges, until you rejoin the throng in Campo di Santa Fosca. Follow Strada Nova eastwards to the Ca' d'Oro, catching your

Above from far left: by the canal; Campo del Ghetto Nuovo.

Below: the Madonna dell'Orto.

Food and Drink 🍴

② AL TIMON
Cannaregio 2754, Fondamenta degli Ormesini (Guglie ferry stop); tel: 041-524 6066; Tue–Sun; €
A beautiful canalside setting and laid-back atmosphere make this a favourite. The kitchen serves three or four hot dishes a day, plus salads and delicious *crostini*. Come back later if you're in the mood for late-night folk music or singalongs.

③ LA CANTINA
Cannaregio 3689, Campo San Felice; tel: 041-522 8258; Tue–Sat; €€
Feasts of charcuterie, cheeses, carpaccio, seafood platters, sweet prawn scampi, bean soups and bruschetta, matched by fine wines. Local mutterings about slow service are forgotten when set against the moody but inspirational chef.

④ ALLA VEDOVA
Cannaregio 3912, Ramo Ca' d'Oro; tel: 041-528 5324; Fri–Wed, closed Sun lunch; €€€€
This atmospheric, time-worn inn is known for its wines and hearty *cicchetti*, and, unlike many of its ilk, is friendly towards *foresti* (outsiders). Full seafood meals and pasta dishes are also on offer. Book in advance.

San Michele

San Michele, site of the city cemetery, is easily identified from the mainland by its solemn cypress trees. As the island closest to Venice, it is served by ferries from the Fondamente Nuove. Formerly a prison island, it was Napoleon who decreed that the dead should be brought here, away from the crowded city. The rambling cemetery is lined with gardens stacked with simple memorials or domed family mausoleums. Here lie the tombs of dogal families, obscure diplomats and plague victims, along with such illustrious figures as Stravinsky, Ezra Pound and Diaghilev. Famous foreigners are allowed to rest in peace, but more modest souls tend to be evicted – after 10 years their remains are exhumed and placed in permanent storage boxes. By the landing stage, the cemetery's focal point is the cool, austere Renaissance church of San Michele in Isola. A trip to this peaceful and remote spot is haunting and memorable.

Above from left:
intricate ceiling detail in Santa Maria dei Miracoli; the jewel-like Renaissance exterior of Santa Maria dei Miracoli, a favourite for Venetian weddings; Murano is famous for its glass and colourful facades.

Above: the Gesuiti peeking out from between Venetian town houses; fountain on the Fondamente di Cannaregio.

Venetians' Venice
Cannaregio is the second-largest neighbourhood in Venice (Castello is the biggest), and has the highest population (about 20,000).

breath in a quirky Cannaregio *bacaro* such as **La Cantina**, see ⑪③, or **Alla Vedova**, see ⑪④ *(p.77)*.

The **Ca' d'Oro** ❺, one of the finest palaces on the Grand Canal, is home to the **Franchetti Gallery** (Calle Ca' d'Oro 3932; tel: 041-522 2349; www. cadoro. org; Mon 8.15am–2pm, Tue–Sun 8.15am–7.15pm; charge), a collection of Renaissance treasures. The most prized piece is Mantegna's *St Sebastian*; Tullio Lombardo's delightful marble *Double Portrait*, inspired by ancient funerary reliefs, is also worth singling out. The *portego* is a showcase of sculpture and opens onto the Grand Canal. The palace interior suffered barbaric restoration in the mid-19th century, but still offers fantastic views of the Grand Canal. Viewing the exterior from the Grand Canal, however, you can see why the filigree facade of the Ca' d'Oro is one of the city's great showpieces *(see p.37)*.

Coming out of the Ca' d'Oro, turn right back onto the Strada Nova for the bustling *campo* and church of **SS Apostoli** ❻ (8am–noon, 5–7pm; free), which contains a painting by Tiepolo and an exquisite marble relief of St Sebastian by Tullio Lombardo.

THE GESUITI

Take the northern exit out of the *campo*, behind the church, and you'll come to a small square. At the end of Calle del Manganer, take a left, crossing two bridges until you reach the **Campo dei Gesuiti**. The large ex-monastery of the Jesuits on your right, with bricked-up

windows, was once used as a barracks and is awaiting restoration.

A little further along is the **Gesuiti** ❼ (10am–noon, 4–6pm; free), an extravagant Jesuit church founded in 1714: the interior is a riot of gilded stucco and lavishly sculpted green-and-white marble. Titian's *Martyrdom of St Lawrence* hangs above the first altar on the left.

Just north of the church stretch fine lagoon views from the Fondamente Nuove. Depending on the light, these seemingly remote northern quays can look bleak and washed out or moodily magnificent. If time allows, consider a detour to the cemetery island of San Michele *(see p.77)* by taking the 41 or 42 vaporetto towards Murano for one stop.

SANTA MARIA DEI MIRACOLI

For your final destination, head out of Campo dei Gesuiti the way you came in, walk as far as Calle Muazzo, then follow the signs for Ospedale SS Giovanni e Paolo and Santa Maria dei Miracoli through Campo S. Canzian until you reach Campo S. Maria.

Across the bridge and to the right is the ornate Renaissance church of **Santa Maria dei Miracoli** ❽ (Campo Santa Maria dei Miracoli; Mon–Sat 10am–5pm; Chorus Church, *see p.101*; charge). Rising sheer from the water, the facade offers a dazzling display of marble. Inside, the surfaces are a vision of pale pinks and silvery greys, and pilasters adorned with interlaced flowers, mythical creatures and cavorting mermaids.

MURANO, BURANO AND TORCELLO

Spend a day exploring this trio of lagoon islands. Watch glass-blowing in Murano, wander the canal banks of psychedelic Burano, the friendliest island, and be stirred by Torcello, once the principal settlement of Venice.

MURANO

The island of Murano is sometimes described as a mini-Venice. It cannot match the city for splendour but, like Venice, it is made up of islands and divided by canals, lined with mansions and *palazzi*. It even has its own Grand Canal. But Murano's *raison d'être* has always been the making of glass. As early as the 7th century a glass industry was established near Venice. In the late 13th century the factories were moved to Murano to avoid the hazards of fire from the open furnaces.

Murano glassmakers enjoyed rare privileges, but their craft was a closely guarded secret, and the makers left the shores of Venice on pain of death. Even so, many of them were lured abroad in the 16th century. Those who were discovered, including a few who divulged their secrets to the court of Louis XIV, were condemned to death. Today about 60 percent of the glass produced here is exported. The characteristics of the local glass are deep, bright colours and ornate design.

It's easy to get to the island independently *(see Points to Note in box)*. To avoid the pressure from pushy glass vendors, wait until the **Museo stop ❶** on

DISTANCE 5km (3¼ miles)
TIME A full day
START Museo vaporetto, Murano
END Museo dell'Estuario, Torcello
POINTS TO NOTE

Buy a vaporetto pass as you will need to use several different boats. To reach the starting point, take vaporetto 41 or 42 from Fondamente Nuove or San Zaccaria (both also stop at San Michele). Avoid weekends, when the islands are packed. Beware of free trips offered by touts near Piazza San Marco, who are paid a hefty commission for each tourist brought to a showroom. Hence the pressure to buy and the high prices.

Navigating the Lagoon
Many sections of the lagoon are unnavigable because of the mudflats and sandbanks, but skilled boatmen can weave through the shifting channels and sandbars, guided by the *bricole* – distinctive navigational markers.

Murano before getting off. Signs indicate the **Museo del Vetro ❷** (Glass Museum, Fondamenta Giustinian 8; tel: 041-739 586; www.museicivici veneziani.it; Thur–Tue 10am–6pm, winter until 5pm; charge), containing an eclectic collection of Venetian glass in a 15th-century palazzo. A prize piece is the Coppa Barovier (Barovier being one of a dynasty of Muranese glassmakers) – a 15th-century wedding chalice adorned with allegorical love scenes.

SS Maria e Donato

Leaving the museum, turn left and follow Fondamenta Giustinian for the basilica of **SS Maria e Donato** ❸ (Campo San Donato; 9am–noon, 3.30–7pm, closed Sun am; free). Founded in the 7th century and remodelled in the Veneto-Byzantine style, it is the finest church on Murano. Despite heavy-handed restoration, it retains some outstanding features: the colonnaded apse with decorative brick-work on the canalside; the 12th-century mosaic *pavimento*, adorned with medieval motifs and animals; the ship's keel roof; and the mosaic of the *Madonna and Child*.

Fondamenta Longa

Retrace your steps to the Museo ferry stop, follow the Fondamenta Longa along Murano's own Canal Grande and cross the Ponte Vivarini (some-times called Ponte Longo), named after a 15th-century family of painters who lived on Murano. From the bridge you can see the **Palazzo da Mula** (on the far bank to your right), one of Murano's few surviving grand mansions.

Fondamenta dei Vetrai

Across the bridge to the left is the Gothic **San Pietro Martire** ❹ (Fondamenta dei Vetrai; 9am–noon, 3–6pm, closed Sun am; free) housing two fine altarpieces by Giovanni Bellini. The interior also contains spectacular Murano glass chandeliers and bottle-glass windows in lovely hues. If feeling hungry, cross the canal via the bridge facing the church into Campo Santo Stefano, and enjoy a meal at **Trattoria Busa alla Torre**, see ⑪①.

Afterwards, amble along the **Fondamenta dei Vetrai**, the heart of the glass-making district. The glassworks and showrooms along the quayside offer a chance to admire the glass-blowers' skills. In the morning, market boats selling fresh produce along the canal add to the busy scene. If you

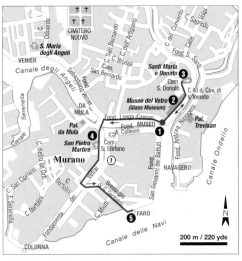

Food and Drink 🍴

① TRATTORIA BUSA ALLA TORRE
Murano, Campo Santo Stefano 3 (Faro ferry stop); tel: 041-739 662; lunch only; €€
This classic Venetian seafood restaurant has been an inn since 1420 and a wine store since the 12th century. Clams, fish grills and lagoon vegetables are generally reliable, as are *sarde in saor* (classic Venetian sweet and sour sardines).

haven't yet seen a glass-blowing display, be lured into one of the workshops (steel yourself for the inevitable sales pitch, and beware of imitations, *see margin p.80*). With incredible skill the maestro blows the blob of molten glass, then with a spatula and a pair of pincers, twists, turns, pinches and flattens it into the shape of an animal or bird.

To continue to Burano, cross the canal at Ponte de Mezo and take Viale Bressagio across the square. This leads to the **Murano Faro stop ❺**, and vaporetto LN for the 30-minute ride.

BURANO

Burano is a splash of colour in a bleak lagoon, dispelling any mournfulness with its parade of colourful fishermen's cottages and bobbing boats. Burano also makes a cheery lunch stop en route to Torcello, its polar opposite, or a dinner stop on the way back from Torcello. Naturally hospitable, the islanders are increasingly known for their Slow Food inns rather than for their lacemaking and fishing traditions.

From the **landing stage ❻**, mill down via Marcello, past brightly painted houses. Turn left at the end of the street and cross over the bridge, turning left again onto the Fondamenta degli Assassini. To view the most colourful courtyard on the island, take the tiny alley marked Via al Gattolo. At No. 339, **Casa Bepi ❼** has a dazzling multicoloured, geometrical facade.

If hungry, make your way to Via Baldassare Galuppi, the main street, named after the composer who was

Buyer Beware
The lace and linen
stalls on the island
vie for attention
but most of these
tablecloths and
napkins have been
factory-made in Asia.
As with Murano glass,
beware of imitations.

born here. Try either the **Trattoria da Romano**, see ②, or **Al Gatto Nero**, see ①③. Stick to fish and you will not be disappointed.

Lace and Linen

The downfall of the Republic led to the inevitable decline of the lace industry, but a revival took place in 1872 when a lacemaking school was founded in an effort to combat local poverty. Today, Burano is one of the last sur-viving centres of handmade lace, and the Buranesi struggle valiantly to keep the tradition alive..

To see authentic Burano lace and the women who make it, visit the revamped **Museo del Merletto** ⑧ (Lace Museum; Piazza Galuppi; tel: 041-730 034; www.museiciviciveneziani.it; Wed–Mon 10am–6pm, until 5pm in winter; charge). Here priceless antique pieces are displayed behind glass.

Mazzorbo

From Burano, cross the wooden footbridge to the more rural island of **Mazzorbo**. At first sight it looks similar to Burano: the same colourful cottages lining the canal. Here too, when not ruining their eyesight poring over lace, the fishermen's wives painted the family homes in psychedelic colours, often adding geometrical motifs over the doorways, and opening inns. But there the similarities end. You soon catch sight of a sluggish canal, a walled vineyard, and a solitary brick bell tower (14th-century).

On the waterfront lies the entrance to **Venissa**, see ①④ the lagoon's last walled vineyard, now at the heart of a model estate encompassing a cosy inn and gourmet restaurant. Venissa is sustainable tourism at its best. The prosecco-making Bisol dynasty has reclaimed the vineyard and planted it with Dorona, the golden grape beloved by the doges, once widely cultivated on the lagoon but now at risk of extinction. After visiting Torcello, try to return to Venissa for dinner as ferries run back to central Venice until late.

Food and Drink

② DA ROMANO
Burano, Via Galuppi 221; tel: 041-730 030; www.daromano.it; Wed–Mon, closed Sun dinner; €€
This welcoming fish restaurant is both hearty and arty. The interior is adorned with paintings donated by visiting artists.

③ AL GATTO NERO
Burano, Via Giudecca 88; tel: 041-730 120, www.gattonero.com; €€
This long-established family-run seafood restaurant is famous for seafood risotto, as well as for lagoon vegetables, such as Sant'Erasmo artichokes, or pasta made with tiny lagoon crabs.

④ VENISSA
Mazzorbo, Fondamenta di Santa Catarina 3; tel: 041-5272 281; (Ferry LN from Fondamenta Nuove to Burano, then cross the footbridge); April–Sept Tue–Sun; www.venissa.it; €€€–€€€€
In a bucolic setting chef Paola Budel showcases sustainable Slow Food, with Adriatic scampi, cuttlefish, and roast bream complemented by baby artichokes and estate figs.

⑤ LOCANDA CIPRIANI
Torcello, Piazza Santa Fosca 29; tel: 041-730 150; www.locandacipriani.com; Feb–Dec Wed–Mon lunch; €€€
This rural retreat, run by the nephew of Arrigo Cipriani, the owner of Harry's Bar, is a local institution. Try the grilled fish, fillet steak or *risotto alla torcellana*. Book in advance.

⑥ AL PONTE DEL DIAVOLO
Torcello, Fondamenta Borgognoni 10; tel: 041-730 401; Mar–Dec Tue–Sun L; €€
This is a hospitable and atmospheric (lunch only) spot, with pasta and seafood dishes predominating.

For now, retrace your steps to the ferry and head for Torcello, a short jaunt from Burano on Line T, which departs every half-hour.

TORCELLO

Torcello, the most remote of these islands (an hour by ferry), is the least populated but, for many, the most resonant. This marshy, unprepossessing spot was the site of the original settlement in the Venetian lagoon. It is hard to believe it was once the centre of a thriving civilisation. In its heyday, Torcello's population was around 20,000, but this figure has fallen to 70. As Venice rose to power, decline set in, trade on Torcello dwindled and the waters silted up. Today the cathedral, church and a couple of *palazzi* are the sole evidence of former splendour. But it is this palpable sense of loss that makes the island such a nostalgic spot.

From the **landing stage** ❾, where the cathedral bell tower soars above the marshland, follow the well-beaten towpath to the centre of civilisation, such as it is. If you arrive at lunch time, enjoy a life-enhancing feast in **Locanda Cipriani**, see ⑪⑤. Hemingway, Queen Elizabeth II, Sir Winston Churchill, Charlie Chaplin and Sophia Loren are just a few who have made the same journey to this celebrated outpost. A less pricey alternative is the rustic **Al Ponte del Diavolo**, see ⑪⑥.

Santa Maria dell'Assunta

Carry on down the same path to where the settlement began: the cathedral of **Santa Maria dell'Assunta** ❿ (Piazza di Torcello; tel; 041-730 119; daily Mar–Oct 10.30am–6pm, Nov–Feb until 5pm; charge, a combined ticket covers the cathedral, bell tower and museum). The oldest church in Venice, it was founded in AD639 but rebuilt between the 9th and 11th centuries. Note the foundations of the original baptistery on your left as you enter and the massive, 11th-century stone slabs acting as shutters on the south side of the cathedral.

Above from far left: colourful Burano; golden mosaics in Santa Maria dell'Assunta.

Burano Lace
Lacemaking was a traditional occupation for fishermen's wives, whose menfolk were away at sea. In the 16th century, Burano lace was in great demand, so much so that the court of Louis XIV closed its doors to Venetian lace and created a royal industry of its own. Every means possible was used to steal the industry from La Serenissima, by inducing women to leave Burano and providing them with workshops that recreated Venetian designs.

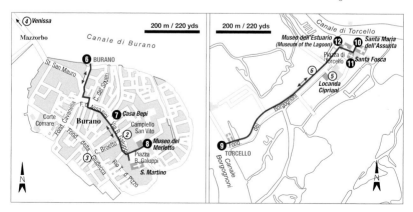

Attila's Seat
According to local
folklore, if single
people sit on Attila's
Seat they will be
married within
the year.

Torcello Lament
Like Ruskin, most
writers strike an
elegiac note when
faced with the
collapse of this early
Venetian settlement:
'The lament of many
human voices mixed
with the fretting of the
waves on the ridges
of the sand.'
However, if you are
fortunate, and the
crowds are in
abeyance, you may
share George Sand's
enchantment with
Torcello: 'The air was
balmy and only the
song of cicadas
disturbed the religious
hush of the morning.'

The interior is impressive, and its lovely mosaics are among the oldest and finest in Italy. Most striking of all is *The Virgin and Child*, set against a glowing gold background in the dome of the central apse. Covering the western wall is *The Last Judgement*, a massive narrative mosaic. From this end admire the church in its entirety: the slender marble columns, the wooden tie-beams and the roodscreen carved with peacocks, lions and flowers, surmounted by a frieze of 15th-century paintings. Sadly, the bell tower is currently closed for restoration so stirring views of the lagoon will have to wait for another time.

Other Highlights

The church of **Santa Fosca** ⓫ (daily 10am–4.30pm), which adjoins the cathedral, was built in the 11th century to enshrine the body of Santa Fosca, a Christian martyr. Close by, the weathered stone chair known as **Attila's Seat** is associated with the king of the Huns. On the opposite side of the piazza, the **Museo di Torcello** ⓬ (Tue–Sun 10.30am– 5pm; charge) contains archaeological finds and salvaged Byzantine mosaics. Dusk, when the sun is setting over the lagoon, is a beautiful time to return to Venice, unless you go back to Venissa for dinner and catch a late ferry back.

The Minor Islands

As your boat takes you through the northern lagoon, past Murano, and on towards Burano and Torcello, you will pass a number of small islands. On your right for most of the journey from Murano to Burano, you can see the marshy islets and main island of Sant'Erasmo, whose fruit and vegetables end up in the Rialto market. First, however, you will pass Le Vignole, an island where, during the summer, many Venetians stop to swim and eat at the delicious rustic restaurant located here (Alle Vignole; Apr–Sept Tue–Sun). Both Le Vignole and Sant'Erasmo are accessible by vaporetto No. 13 from the Fondamente Nuove, but service is sporadic. The ferry swings left around the deserted island of San Giacomo in Palude, one of many abandoned in the 1960s. To the right, in the distance, a dark cluster of cypresses marks the romantic island of San Francesco del Deserto, where St Francis is said to have retreated in 1220. The island is not accessible by public transport, so you will need to hire a water taxi or a boat from the fishermen on Burano. The monastery has recently been renovated, and the Franciscan friars offer guided visits (tel: 041-528 6863; www.isola-sanfrancescodeldeserto.it; Tue–Sun 9–11am, 3–5pm; donation appreciated). Sant'Erasmo and San Francesco del Deserto are market garden islands, especially known for asparagus and artichokes. Their fresh produce is brought in daily to the Rialto markets.

THE LIDO

Leave the sights of the city, catch a vaporetto to Venice's main bathing resort and cool off in the waters of the Adriatic. Enjoy its Belle Epoque architecture and maybe go for a gentle cycle ride along the sea wall.

The long strip of land, around 11km (7 miles), protecting the Venetian lagoon from the Adriatic Sea, was Italy's first Lido. In the 19th century, when it was no more than a spit of sand, Byron, Shelley and other Romantics came to escape the city, riding along its white sands and bathing in its waters. By the turn of the 20th century it was one of the most fashionable resorts in Europe, and the name was subsequently applied to dozens of bathing resorts throughout the world.

The Lido may have lost its cachet since *Death in Venice* was set here, but is now in vogue once more, with iconic hotels and beaches revamped, and the creation of a new marina and yacht club. Given the resolutely urban nature of Venice, a summer dip at the Lido still provides a cooling-off experience, while the 15-minute ferry ride across the lagoon is a breeze. And helping preserve this landscape is the MOSE mobile dam, being constructed across the Lido entrance to the lagoon.

JEWISH CEMETERY AND SAN NICOLÒ

All ferries arrive at **Piazzale Santa Maria Elisabetta ❶**, where the sight of cars may come as a culture shock. From here, you can take a bus or taxi,

DISTANCE 6km (4 miles)
TIME A full day
START Piazzale Santa Maria Elisabetta
END Grand Hotel Excelsior
POINTS TO NOTE
Unless indulging in a motor launch, take a ferry (Nos 1, 2, 51, LN) from Riva degli Schiavoni to the Lido. Nos 1, 2, 51, and 61 also go from Piazzale Roma. Young families usually love the Lido but avoid summer Sundays, when the Venetians flock here.

hire a bike or walk to the eastern side of the island via the **Riviera Santa Maria Elisabetta**. The first landmark is the Tempio Votivo, commemorating the victims of both world world wars. Many of the houses that line this seafront stretch were built in the 1920s, and reflect the fashion for reinterpreting Byzantine and Gothic Venetian architecture.

Jewish Cemetery

Further along the seafront (after Riviera San Nicolò) is the **Antico Cimitero Ebraico ❷** (Old Jewish Cemetery; entrance on Via Cipro; tel: 041-715 5359; www.museoebraico.it; Apr–Sept guided tours in English, but no fixed

Bike Rental
As you'll be covering quite a distance, you might consider renting a bike for the day. Try Gardin Anna Valli (Piazzale S.M. Elisabetta 2A; tel: 041-760 005) or Lido on Bike (Gran Viale S.M. Elisabetta 21; tel: 041-526 8019). Bike rental normally costs between €12 and €20 a day, depending on the bike (there are also tandems) and there are deals for families renting more than one bike.

times; enquire at the Jewish Museum). The Jewish community was granted use of this land in 1386, which reflects the status of Jews in Venice at the time – segregated even in death, they were rowed down the Canale degli Ebrei to the Lido, the cemetery for outcasts.

San Nicolò

Continuing along the lagoon shore, you will reach the church and Benedictine monastery of **San Nicolò** ❸ (Piazzale San Nicolò; 9am–noon, 4–7pm; free). From the church there are good views of the **Fortezza di Sant' Andrea**, a huge bastion on the island of Le Vignole built between 1535 and 1549 to guard the main entrance of the lagoon. Once a year, the doge would attend Mass at San Nicolò after the annual Marriage of the Sea ritual in the Porto di Lido. From the ceremonial stage barge he would cast a gold ring into the water, symbolising the marriage of Venice with the sea.

Nowadays Venice needs more than the doge's blessing to save it from serious floods so the city has turned to MOSE (Moses), the flood barrier being erected in the lagoon nearby. The emerging mobile dam can be visited on boat trips (tel: 041-529 3600).

After pondering the fate of Venice, head back towards the Jewish Ceme-

---

Food and Drink

① TRATTORIA ANDRI

Via Lepanto 21; tel: 041-526 5482; open Wed–Sun; €€

This pleasant canalside trattoria may tempt you away from the beach with its straightforward lagoon cuisine, based on seafood. Tuck into hearty platters of grilled or fried fish, as well as seafood salads and a refreshing house sorbet to finish.

② AURORA BEACH CLUB

Lungomare Gabriele d'Annunzio 20x, tel: (+39) 335 526 8013; €

By day, this is an enjoyable beach club with simple snacks and bar food. The mood changes at sunset when a funky beach scene sets in, with cocktails, live DJs, possibly an open-air cinema, and partying until late.

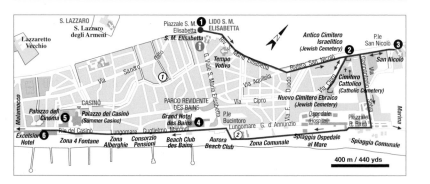

tery, turning left down via Giannantonio Selva to the beach. For lunch, depending on the season, choose between a proper Venetian affair at **Trattoria Andri**, see ⑨①, or the laidback **Aurora Beach Club**, see ⑨②.

THE SEASIDE

The over-crowded, free public beach in front of Piazzale Ravà gives way to more desirable private beaches further west (charge), including the one opposite **Hôtel des Bains e Residenze** and, for a party scene, **Aurora Beach Club**, where you can also treat yourself to a candy-striped *cabana* and sunbed *(see margin, right)*.

Lungomare G. Marconi

The smarter stretch of beach abuts **Lungomare G. Marconi**, the boulevard with the best hotels and beaches, notably the manicured shore facing **Hôtel des Bains ❹**. This is the Lido's most glamorous landmark, immortalised by Thomas Mann in his 1912 novella *Death in Venice*. The book tells the story of Gustav von Aschenbach, an author with writer's block who comes to Venice for a restorative stay; but the lagoon's heady, claustrophobic, muggy setting sparks a mid-life crisis, when von Aschenbach falls in love with a Polish boy also staying at the hotel; Italian director Luchino Visconti's 1971 screen adaptation, starring Dirk Bogarde as Aschenbach and filmed on the island, evokes the Lido's *dolce vita* days. The good times should roll again in 2013, after the Art Deco Des Bains

is transformed into a boutique hotel and luxury apartments, with a chic beach club leading eastwards to what will be the largest marina in the Adriatic.

Lido Palazzi

Further along the seafront, the former **Palazzo del Casinò** (now a congress centre) and **Palazzo del Cinema ❺** embody the Fascist architecture of the 1930s. In early September, celebrities flock to the latter for the Film Festival *(see p.23 and below)*.

End your seaside outing by admiring the exuberant, restored late 19th- to early 20th-century neo-Byzantine **Excelsior Hotel ❻**. Bid farewell to the Lido in the hotel's chic Blue Bar, reportedly home to Venice's best Martinis.

Above from far left: the bronzed and beautiful; the Liberty Restaurant at the Hôtel des Bains.

Beach Babes
For the full Italian beach scene, join the bronzed Euro-set at the Lido beach clubs. If you arrive after 2pm on weekdays the beach fees are negligible and include parasol and beach bed. To avoid paying at all, stay by the water's edge. Or hire a bike and set off for Alberoni at the southern tip, with a pine forest and Blue Flag status.

Venice Film Festival

Venice is the world's oldest film festival and now rivals Cannes in prestige and the Côte d'Azur in terms of glitz. Early on, the festival celebrated such vintage performances as Greta Garbo in *Anna Karenina* (1935) and Laurence Olivier's *Hamlet* (1948), while directors of the calibre of John Ford and Auguste Renoir brought glamour to the Lido. The glory days coincided with New Wave cinema in the 1960s, a fame sealed by the movies of Godard, Pasolini, Tarkovsky and Visconti. Recently, the festival has gone all out for Hollywood glitz, and big names still get top billing, even if worthy art-house winners tend to triumph in the end.

Unlike Cannes, the Venice Film Festival increasingly attracts hordes of local people, who head to the Lido for the numerous public screenings. Venetian movie buffs are also delighted at the Lido's facelift, including the revamping of the Palazzo del Cinema. Glamour has made a comeback.

VENICE IN A DAY

Around 7 million people a year (about half the city's visitors) are day-trippers. If you are among this number and want to do a whistle-stop tour, follow this route, which pulls together highlights from many of the other walks.

Above: on the Grand Canal; Rialto Bridge.

Extending the Tour

Have more time? You can always add a more in-depth exploration of southern Dorsoduro *(see walk 7, p.57)* or head back towards San Rocco and take in the church of the Frari and the San Polo district *(see walk 9, p.65).*

DISTANCE 3km (2 miles)
TIME A full day
START/END Stazione Ferroviaria Santa Lucia
POINTS TO NOTE

This walk is designed to last from 9am–5pm, allowing time for meals and snacks. If you are travelling to and from Venice by train, leave plenty of time to get back to the station – it is a 30-minute ride from San Tomà via vaporetto No. 1, or 15 minutes via vaporetto No. 2. It is a good idea to buy a 12-hour vaporetto ticket (€18), since you will be using this mode of transport several times during the day. You can easily start at Piazzale Roma, where you can catch the No. 1 vaporetto. To condense the day due to time constraints, travel via vaporetto No. 2, which makes fewer stops.

Though one can only scratch the surface of Venice's immense heritage in one day, this walk will find you spending a morning in the monumental Piazza San Marco with an afternoon in a quintessential neighbourhood square that is popular with a local crowd. This mix aims to whet your appetite for Venice and make you thirst for a return visit.

GRAND CANAL AND RIALTO

Start at the **Stazione Ferroviaria Santa Lucia ❶** (Train Station), taking either the No. 1 vaporetto on the 13-minute ride to the Rialto Mercato stop. Take in the fantastic architecture found along the Grand Canal, looking out for ornate tracery on the Gothic palace of Ca' d'Oro *(see p.37 and p.77).*

If you book in advance, you might have time for an hour's **gondola ride** with the only female gondolier *(see 52).* Known as the Gondoliera, Alex Hai provides a mysterious, personalised tour, attuned to Venice as a visceral experience of sound, secrets, water and light.

Rialto Markets

Disembark at **Rialto Mercato ❷**, walk straight ahead into Campo Bella Vienna, and, if you arrive on any day other than Sunday, drink in the sights, smells, and sounds of the famous Rialto market *(see p.70).* The Rialto, the first area in Venice to be populated, has long been the commercial heart of the lagoon.

First, turn left and take the time to wander through the Erberia as well, with its canalside bars *(see p.71),* which is a pleasant stop for photographs.

Heading back into Campo Bella Vienna, turn right onto the Casaria, which will take you through the produce stalls and toward the two covered **Pescheria** ❸ (Fish Market; Tue–Sat; *see p.71*). The market makes an inviting place to stock up on snacks for the next leg of your trip.

From the Pescheria, take any street on your left then head south down Ruga degli Speziali, the street of the spice traders, where you may catch a whiff of fresh coffee beans and the spices that are still sold from an ancient spice shop. If you want to have a coffee or perhaps some traditional *cicchetti*, wander over to tiny **All'Arco**, see ⑪①, a great place for a pit stop.

Rialto Bridge

Returning to Ruga degli Speziali, continue south down Ruga dei Orefici, past the church of San Giacomo di Rialto (the oldest church in Venice, *see p.72–3*), and over the **Ponte di Rialto** ❹ *(see p.73)*, the only permanent crossing point on the Grand Canal until the 19th century, making it an important location for merchants.

Fondaco dei Tedeschi

Straight ahead, the building slightly to the left is the **Fondaco dei Tedeschi** ❺ *(see p.73)*. At one time the Germans used this building as their warehouse, mercantile offices and as lodging for Germans trading in the lagoon.

Above: panoramic view of the Castello district with the Laguna Veneta on the horizon.

Food and Drink

① ALL'ARCO

San Polo 436, Calle dell'Occhialer; tel: 041-520 5666; Mon–Sat; €

In the warren of the Rialto, this tiny *bacaro* sets out a few tables, which are invariably fought over by regular customers. The friendly father-and-son team serve some of the best (and best-value) *cicchetti* in town, as well as delicious *crostini*.

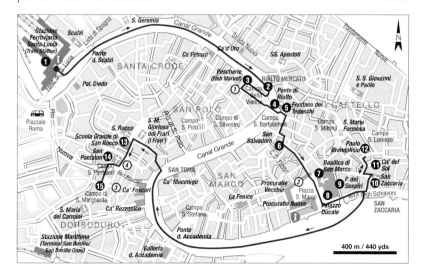

Lunch Early

When planning what time to stop for lunch, make sure you don't wait too long. Many of the smaller restaurants close between lunch and dinner sittings, so you might miss out.

Above: sculpture of Adam on the Palazzo Ducale; Bridge of Sighs.

The Waterways Demystified

Be sure to buy the right day-long water transport pass (including the Grand Canal): currently €20 for 24 hours; €18 for 12 hours; €7 for an hour's journey. Passes are discounted if pre-booked on www. veniceconnected.com *(for more details see margin note, p.36).*

SAN MARCO

Coming straight off the bridge down Salizzada Pio X brings you to the San Marco district *(see p.28 and p.46),* most famous for its Piazza, but also containing many other fine attractions.

San Salvadore

Turn right down the Marzarietta (also known as Via 2 Aprile), until you reach the church of **San Salvadore** ❻ (Campo San Salvadore; Mon–Sat 9am–noon, 3–6pm, Sun 3–7pm; free). The church, built in the 16th century, contains two lovely works by Titian, an *Annunciation,* in the third altar to the left, and *The Transfiguration,* at the high altar. The tomb of Caterina Cornaro, queen of Cyprus, can be found in the south transept. Caterina's fate outlines the use of marriage as a political pawn. As a young girl she was married to the king of Cyprus, a move made to seal the links between Venice and the country. When her husband died in 1474 – some say at the design of the Venetians – she inherited his

---

Food and Drink 🍽

② GRANCAFFÈ AND RISTORANTE QUADRI

Procuratie Vecchie, Piazza San Marco; tel: 041-522 2105; summer daily, Tue–Sun in winter; €€ café, €€€€ restaurant

On the floor above the famous Grancaffè Quadri, founded in 1638 there is now an elegant gourmet restaurant run by a 3-star Michelin chef – with views over San Marco to match. Booking is essential.

---

kingdom. She was eventually 'persuaded' by Venice to cede Cyprus, and, in exchange, was rewarded with the small Veneto town of Asolo.

Coming out of the church, take the Mercerie San Salvadore south as far as Piazza San Marco, reached through the archway of the clock tower, the Torre dell'Orologio *(see p.35).*

Piazza San Marco

You have now arrived in what is the only square worthy of the title piazza in Venice. Napoleon called it 'the most elegant drawing room in Europe', although this does make one wonder why he then proceeded to hack down one end of it – now the site of the Ala Napoleonica (Napoleonic Wing) – destroying in the process Sansovino's church of San Geminiano.

If you have time, you could enjoy a spritz, a traditional aperitif, or a prosecco, at one of the cafes on the square, such as **Caffè Quadri**, see ⑪②, or its rival, **Caffè Florian** *(see p.29).*

Basilica San Marco

Next stop is the **Basilica San Marco** ❼ (tel: 041-522 5205; daily 9.45am–4.45pm; free, but charge for Museo Marciano, Pala d'Oro and Treasury; *see p.28).* To maximise your time, reserve tickets with Alata (www. alata.it). Alternatively, and if you have luggage, check it in at the nearby Ateneo Basso (just off Piazzetta Leoncina on Calle San Basso), and you will get a tag that allows you to skip the queue.

Once the private chapel of the Venetian doge, the basilica is decorated to

impress. Visits last only about 10 minutes, as you are shuffled along a roped-off route, but you will still have time to take in the impressive mosaic interior. Make sure you pop into the Museo Marciano, where you can view the bronze horses originally brought back from Constantinople to crown the main door of the basilica (the ones currently outside are copies), as well as fantastic views over the square.

Palazzo Ducale

You don't really have time on this tour to go into the **Palazzo Ducale** ❽ *(see p.32)*, but you can, of course, still admire the glorious Gothic facade, where white stone and pink marble are used to dazzling effect. If you have time, take a closer look at some of the column capitals that ring the building. In the left-hand corner, closest to the Basilica San Marco, is a depiction of the *Judgement of Solomon*. Other capitals depict professions, animals and goods that were typical in the Republic of Venice, all showing the use of architecture to promote civic glory.

Exit the square in the direction of the lagoon, passing two columns topped by San Teodoro, the former patron saint of Venice, and the Winged Lion, the symbol of St Mark, the current patron saint of the city.

The Molo and Bridge of Sighs

Turn left onto the quayside, known as the Molo, and standing on the crowded Ponte della Paglia, you will catch a glimpse of the restored **Ponte dei Sospiri** ❾ (Bridge of Sighs; *see p.34*),

constructed to transport criminals from the prisons to the adjoining law courts.

While strolling east along the Molo, the waterfront closest to the Basilica, look across the lagoon for views of San Giorgio Maggiore *(see p.62)*.

CASTELLO

After crossing the Ponte del Vin, duck under the second *sottoportego* on your left and you will soon find yourself in

Above: people-watching on Piazza San Marco.

Below: the grandiose Sala del Maggior Consiglio in the Palazzo Ducale.

Above: interior of the Ca' del Sol mask workshop, on the Fondamenta dell'Osmarin.

Below: the Riva degli Schiavoni, the waterfront southeast of Piazza San Marco.

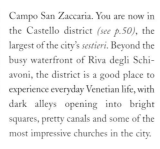

Campo San Zaccaria. You are now in the Castello district *(see p.50)*, the largest of the city's *sestieri*. Beyond the busy waterfront of Riva degli Schiavoni, the district is a good place to experience everyday Venetian life, with dark alleys opening into bright squares, pretty canals and some of the most impressive churches in the city.

San Zaccaria

Much of the land here was once owned by the convent of San Zaccaria, a nunnery that took in the most privileged women in Venetian society, often against their will. Drop into the church of **San Zaccaria 🔟** (Mon–Sat 10am–noon, 4–6pm, Sun 4–6pm; charge; *see p.50*), especially to view the moving *Sacra Conversazione* by Giovanni Bellini, in the first altar on the left.

Mask-Makers

One cannot appreciate Venice without also appreciating the strong history of craftsmanship in the city. Leave the square by the archway in the northern corner, turn right into Campo San Provolo, under a *sottoportego*, and you will arrive at the Fondamenta dell'Osmarin. On the right you will see **Ca' del Sol 🔟**, at No. 4964. This mask workshop carries on the long-standing tradition of hand-crafting papier mâché masks, often based on characters from the *commedia dell'arte (see p.69)*. The idea of anonymity created by the masks appealed to the Venetians, especially during carnival, since it allowed classes to mingle freely.

Gondola Workshops

Just across the street, down the narrow Calle Corte Rota, you will find the workshop of **Paolo Brandolisio 🔟** (No. 4725). Paolo is a *remèri*, the name for an artisan who creates *forcole* (the sculptural oarlock necessary for rowing gondolas) and oars. This is one of just four Venetian workshops that produce this part of the gondola. The *forcola* is formed from an aged trunk of wood, and its finely sculptured shape allows for the correct movement of the oar.

Don't expect your questions answered unless you intend to buy a miniature oarlock as a souvenir, but you can certainly watch from the doorway. However, if you catch the artisans during downtime, they may be happy to answer questions.

At this point, retrace your steps to the Molo, then walk slightly east, along the

Riva degli Schiavoni. From here, catch the No. 1 or 2 vaporetto from **San Zaccaria** up the Grand Canal to the **San Tomà stop**, enjoying the scenery along the way *(see p.36)*.

SAN POLO

The vaporetto deposits you in the San Polo district, which curves into the left bank of the Grand Canal. It is home to two of the city's greatest sights: the Frari, a huge Franciscan church containing masterpieces by Titian and Bellini, and the Scuola di San Rocco, which we visit next.

Scuola Grande di San Rocco

From the vaporetto landing, go straight ahead and turn right into Campo San Tomà. Follow the signs out of the square to reach Tintoretto's masterpiece, the **Scuola Grande di San Rocco** ⓭ (Salizzada San Rocco; tel: 041-523 4864; www.scuolagrande sanrocco.it; daily Apr–Oct 9.30am– 5.30pm, Nov–Mar 10am–5pm; charge; *see p.65*).

DORSODURO

The remainder of this tour will mostly be spent exploring the western part of the artistic Dorsoduro neighbourhood, fuelled by the infusion of students at the Ca' Foscari University.

Take the Calle Fianco della Scuola beside the Scuola, then cross the bridge and at the end turn left and immediately right into Calle San Pantalon; this brings you into the square of the

same name. **San Pantalon** ⓮ (Campo San Pantalon; Mon–Sat 8–10am, 4–6pm; free) has a huge ceiling fresco by Fumiani. On the left-hand side of the square, close to the canal, note the old slab that lists varieties of fish and the minimum sizes they had to reach before they were allowed to be sold.

Campo di Santa Margherita

Cross the bridge over the Rio Foscari and walk to the **Campo di Santa Margherita** ⓯, a rectangular 'square' bustling with local life. A good spot to relax after an intense day of walking is **Ai Do Draghi**, see ⑪③, right on the square, or **Arca**, see ⑪④, which is back towards San Pantalon.

Once you've had a chance to rest your weary feet and enjoy a spot of people-watching – this area is usually very lively with locals – retrace your steps to the San Tomà vaporetto. To reach the railway station (or the nearby bus station) by boat from here, allow yourself approximately 30 to 40 minutes, and longer for the main cruise terminal.

Above from far left: Carnival in full swing; off the beaten track.

Saving San Marco
Beloved by Venetians, St Mark's bell tower is known as *'il paron de casa'* (the master of the house) but is currently not very masterful. The *campanile* is being reinforced with titanium rods to reinforce the foundations and prevent a second collapse. When the bell tower was reconstructed in 1909, cracks appeared almost immediately as the new and old foundations were mismatched, despite the use of traditional materials and methods, such as placing foundations on a raft of larchwood.

Food and Drink

③ AI DO DRAGHI
Dorsoduro 3665, Calle della Chiesa, Campo Santa Margherita; tel: 041-528 9731; summer daily; winter Fri–Wed; €
With tables spilling out onto the *campo*, this cramped, boisterous bar in the heart of the student district serves a delicious spritz, Veneto wines and tasty *tramezzini* made with brie and speck.

④ ARCA
Dorsoduro 3757, Calle Lunga San Pantalon; tel: 041-524 2236; Mon–Sat until midnight; €–€€
Arca combines a pizzeria with a popular *cicchetteria* that draws in young Venetians.

DIRECTORY

A user-friendly alphabetical listing of practical information,
plus hand-picked hotels and restaurants to suit all budgets
and tastes, and the lowdown on nightlife.

A

AGE RESTRICTIONS

While there is no law limiting the age for drinking alcohol in Italy, there is a law against serving alcohol to minors under 16 in restaurants, bars, etc. The legal driving age is 18, but teenagers aged 14 and over are allowed to drive scooters. One can marry with parental consent at 16 and without at 18.

B

BUDGETING FOR YOUR TRIP

To help with planning the trip, here is a list of approximate prices in euros.

Airport Transfer from Marco Polo. *By road*: public bus (ACTV) €5; taxi €50 (for up to four people). *By water*: Alilaguna public water launch €25 return per person; private water taxi €110–200 one way for four people and luggage.

Entertainment. A concert in a main church costs from €25; Fenice opera tickets from €80. Casino admission €5.

Gondolas. From €80–150 (depending on duration, time of day and services, *see Transport* and *Experiences, below*).

Guided Tours. For walking tour allow around €25 (*see Guides and Tours*).

Food. *Tramezzini* (small sandwiches, at café and bar counters) around €2; *cicchetti* (tapas in wine bars) from €2 each; full meal excluding drinks at inexpensive restaurant €25–30; moderate restaurant €40–5; pizza €12–15; beer €3–5; glass of house wine €2–5.

Hotel. For bed and breakfast per night in high season, including tax: deluxe €400 and above; expensive, €280–400; moderate, €140–280; inexpensive, less than €140.

Lido beaches (paying ones). from around €10 (including sunbed/parasol) but only around €3 after 2pm.

Museums and Attractions. €4–20 but best to buy a museum pass – one for all civic museums costs €18.

Public Transport. Vaporetto: €35 for 3 days, €25 for 36 hours, €20 for 1 day (24 hours); €18 for 12 hours.

C

CLIMATE

Venetian winters are cold, summers are hot, and the weather the rest of the year somewhere in between. The winds off the Adriatic and occasional flooding mean Venice can be damp and chilly, although very atmospheric, between November and March. June, July and August can be stifling – air conditioning is pretty essential for a good night's rest at this time of year.

CLOTHING

A pair of comfortable walking shoes is essential – despite Venice's excellent canal transport network, if you want to sightsee, you'll probably spend most of your time on foot. For summer, pack thin cotton clothing and a light jacket for breezy evening vaporetto rides. When visiting churches, your back and shoulders

should be covered. In winter, pack layers, including a warm coat. Smart hotels lend boots in case of light flooding but bring your own waterproof footwear just in case.

Venice is generally an informal city, but stylish dress is expected at smarter restaurants and piano bars, including at the more elegant hotels. Men must wear a jacket and tie for the Casino.

CRIME AND SAFETY

Although Venice is incredibly safe, pickpockets are not uncommon, especially in crowded areas around the Rialto and San Marco. Carry only what is absolutely necessary; leave passports, airline tickets and all but one credit card in the hotel safe. If nervous, consider a money belt, and be careful on crowded public transport, especially getting on and off the vaporetti, around the train station and in San Marco.

Make photocopies of your passport and other vital documents to facilitate reporting any theft and obtaining replacements. Notify the police as soon as possible of any theft, so that they can give you a statement to file with your insurance claim.

CRUISE VENICE

The **Blue Alilaguna** route (www.alilaguna.it) links the Cruise Terminal to both San Marco and Marco Polo Airport. New cruise terminals reflect the huge popularity of cruising. Even if you only have one day in Venice, reliable transport links will

help you get the most from a fleeting visit. The main Venice Cruise Terminal (**Terminal Venezia Passeggeri**) is close to the 4km (2-mile) causeway that links the historic city with the mainland. Centred on the **Bacino Stazione Marittima (Marittima Basin)**, it handles the largest ships. The additional **San Basilio Terminal** is closer to the main sights, just around the corner in the Giudecca Canal. The **Sette Martiri quays** near the Biennale gardens are mostly used by river cruises and smaller craft. For cruise information, including maps, see: www.vtp.it.

CUSTOMS AND ENTRY REQUIREMENTS

EU citizens: a valid passport or identity card is all that is needed to enter Italy for stays of up to 90 days. Citizens of Australia, Canada, New Zealand and the US require only a valid passport.

Visas. For stays of more than 90 days a visa *(permesso di soggiorno)* or residence permit is required. Regulations change from time to time, so check with the Italian Embassy (www.esteri.it) or in your home country before you travel.

Customs. Free exchange of non-duty-free goods for personal use is allowed between countries within the EU. Refer to your home country's regulating organisation for a current list of import restrictions.

Currency Restrictions. Tourists may bring €10,000 cash (or equivalent in other currency) into the country.

D

DISABLED TRAVELLERS

Accessible Italy
Profits fom
Accessible Italy
go towards funding
much-needed
accessibility
improvements
throughout Italy.

With narrow alleys and stepped bridges, Venice is a challenge, especially if you are not travelling through a specialist tour operator or able to splash out on water taxis. Ideally, book through a specialist foreign operator, or even one on the ground. **Accessible Italy** (tel: +39 378 94 111, www.accessibleitaly.com) provides a list. But there *are* ways of getting around and seeing some of the major sights. For transport tips, see **Venice Connected** (www.veniceconnected.com) and check the 'Accessible Venice' section. As for hotels, avoid the Santa Croce and San Polo areas, which are unsuitable, and ideally opt for a Grand Canal hotel near a ferry stop or a hotel with a free water shuttle. For walks, ramps along the Zattere make this delightful stroll more accessible. If you speak Italian, **Citta per Tutti** has a useful website at www.comune.venezia.it/informahandicap and a branch at Ca' Farsetti, Riva del Carbon, San Marco 4136; tel: 041-274 8144/041-965 5440.

The main (very busy) **tourist office** in the Venice Pavilion *(see p.106)* supplies maps with itineraries marking accessible areas, bridges with ramps for wheelchairs, and toilets for the disabled. Keys to operate the bridges are available from the tourist office, but it can be a saga. Accessible attractions (no differentiation is made between full and partial access) include the Basilica San Marco, Palazzo Ducale, Ca' Rezzonico, and the Frari and La Salute churches.

DRIVING

Venice is a traffic-free zone, and the closest you can get to the centre is Piazzale Roma, where there are two large multistorey car parks and good ferry services (www.asmvenezia.it). There is also a huge multistorey car park on the adjacent island of Tronchetto, the terminal for the car ferry to the Lido, where driving is allowed. Tronchetto, the largest car park in Europe (tel: 041-520 7555; www.veniceparking.it), is linked to Piazzale Roma via the new monorail, called the People Mover. There are also good transport links to the Cruise Terminal. On the mainland at Mestre San Giuliano and Fusina, there are a further two car parks; both have easy bus links to Venice. Although the outdoor car parks are guarded it's sensible not to leave anything of value in your car.

E

ELECTRICITY

The electrical current is 220V, AC, and sockets take two-pin round-pronged plugs. Bring an adaptor *(un adattatore)*, as required.

EMBASSIES AND CONSULATES

Most have lists of English-speaking doctors, lawyers, interpreters, etc.

Australia (Consulate): Via Borgogna 2, Milan tel: 02-776 741, www.italy.embassy.gov.au.

Canada (Consulate): Riviera Ruzzante 25, Padua; tel: 049-876 4833.

New Zealand (Embassy): Via Clitunno 44, Rome; tel: 06-853 7501, www.nzembassy.com.

Republic of Ireland (Embassy): Piazza di Campitelli 3, Rome; tel: 06-697 9121, www.embassyofireland.it.

South Africa (Consulate): Santa Croce 466, Piazzale Roma, Venice; tel: 041-524 1599.

UK (Consulate): Piazzale Donatori di Sangue 2, Mestre; tel: 041-505 5990, www.ukve.it.

US (Consulate): Via Principe Amedeo 2/10, Milan; tel: 02-290 351, milan.usconsulate.gov.

EMERGENCIES

Ambulance: 118; **Fire**: 115; **Carabinieri**: 112 (urgent police action); **Police**: 113

EXPERIENCES

Cookery courses: Chef and foodie expert Countess Enrica Rocca runs full-day cooking classes, including visits to the Rialto market. Courses in very small groups are usually on Tuesdays and cost €280 per person; evening classes on Wednesdays cost €180 and Monday evening wine pairings €200 (tel: + 39 338 634 3839; www.enricarocca.com for further information).

Cycling: While cycling is (sensibly) banned from Central Venice, the Lido makes a perfect cycling destination, if only for a day (or half-day) trip. Bikes can be picked up close to the Lido ferry stop (for details and bike hire companies on the Lido, *see Tour 13*).

Gondola tour with a twist: For an atmospheric, personalised gondola tour with the only female gondolier in Venice, known as *'La Prima Gondoliera'*, contact Alex Hai *(see p.52)*. You even get a bottle of prosecco in the gondola (tel: +39 348 302 9067; email: primagondoliera@gmail.com).

Rowing, Venetian-style: Row Venice teaches Venetian rowing in a matter of hours: standing and facing forward and rowing using a long oar which rests on the special wooden oarlock known as the *forcola* (from €40; contact Jane Caporal, Row Venice, tel: +39 345 241 5266, www.rowvenice.com, mailto:info@rowvenice.com)

Kayaking in Venice or the lagoon: Venice Kayak offers refreshingly untouristy kayak tours around the city and lagoon, including seeing the sights from the water. Day or night paddles from Camping San Nicolò, on the Lido (€100pp per day). (Contact Rene Seidal of Venice Kayak, tel: +39 346 477 1327, www.venicekayak.com.)

Venetian Club: a community-minded 'club' that tempts you to try out ancient Venetian crafts like ceramics or bookbinding: www.thevenetianclub.co.uk.

Above from far left: Palazzo Ducale ceiling; golden mosaics, Basilica San Marco.

Venetian Activities
The experiences listed here are quintessential Venetian activities, but do also see the Guides and Tours section for more tips.

F

FESTIVALS AND EVENTS

These are the main traditional festivities but Venetians love an excuse for a party or a water pageant so expect myriad smaller events.

February
Carnevale (Carnival). These pre-Lenten festivities are celebrated in unrivalled style in Venice *(see p.20–1)*.

May
Festa della Sensa, Ascension Day. Venice celebrates its 'marriage with the sea' in a ceremony during which the mayor throws a ring into the water between St Mark's and the Lido island. There's also a regatta pageant and rowing races.

Vogalonga. On 12 June. Hundreds of boats descend upon the waterways for a colourful 30km (18-mile) race (www.vogalonga.it).

June
Venice Biennale is a major modern art fair held from June–October in odd-numbered years, including in the Biennale pavilions, gardens, and in the old Arsenale (www.labiennale.org)

July
Festa del Redentore, on the third Saturday of July, celebrates the city's deliverance from the plague in 1567 with fireworks and a lagoon procession (www.comunevenezia.it).

September
Venice Film Festival. Usually the last day of August and first week of September: (www.labiennale.org).

Regatta Storica. First Sunday. The Historical Regatta starts with the water pageant on the Grand Canal, followed by races in traditional boats.

G

GUIDES AND TOURS

The tourist office *(see below)* can supply a list of qualified tour guides if you want a personal tour of a particular site or on a specialist aspect of Venice. All year round there are standard tours (book through hotels and travel agencies), including a two-hour walking tour of San Marco, taking in the Basilica and the Palazzo Ducale; a two-hour walking a tour covering the Frari and the Grand Canal; a three-hour islands tour; and even a ghost walk. Also see **Experiences** *(p.99)*.

Accademia Gallery: for booking tickets at set times or for booking individual art tours (tel: 041-520 0345).

Brenta Canal cruise: a cruise to Padua aboard the 200-seater *Burchiello* (www.burchiello.it) motorboat, traces the lives of Venetian nobility in their summer villas; book through travel agencies. The return journey is by coach.

Chorus Churches: Chorus (tel: 041-275 0462,) promotes the preservation

**Above from far
left:** detail from the
front of the Basilica
San Marco; view
to San Marco from
Castello, along the
Riva degli Schiavoni.

of the city's churches and offers guided tours from Mar–Jun and Sept–Dec to a number of churches. An unbeatable discount pass (€10) covers entrance to 15 venues, and may be bought at any of the participating churches.

Flights over Venice: the Aeroclub di Venezia (tel: 041-526 0808) at San Nicolò airport on the Lido offers hour-long flights.

Lagoon tours: Destination Venice offer made-to-measure explorations of the lagoon and islands, along with individual guided walks, and Venetian-style rowing lessons. Campo San Luca, San Marco 4590, tel 041-528 3547, www.destination-venice.com.

St Mark's and the Doge's Palace: Free tours of the Basilica in summer, while the **Secret Itinerary** (Itinerari Segreti; booking essential on www.museicivi-civeneziane.it, tel: 848 082 000) shows you the ins and outs of life at the Palazzo Ducale *(see walk 1)*.

HEALTH AND MEDICAL CARE

EU residents: obtain an EHIC (European Health Insurance Card), available online at www.ehic.org.uk, which provides emergency medical/hospital *(ospedale)* treatment by reciprocal agreement.

For US citizens: if your private health insurance policy does not cover you while abroad (Medicare does not have coverage outside the US), take out a short-term policy before leaving home. **Medical emergencies**: Ask at your hotel if you need a doctor/dentist who speaks English. Your consulate *(see p.98)* should also have lists. The **Guardia Medica** (tel: 041-529 4060) is a call-out service operating from 8pm–8am.

Many doctors at Venice's only hospital, next to San Zanipolo, speak English; tel: 041-529 4111 (and ask for *pronto soccorso* – A&E/casualty).

Mosquitoes: a big nuisance in Venice in summer. Maybe take a small plug-in machine that burns a tablet emitting fumes that are noxious to them. Take cream with you to soothe bites.

Pharmacies: *Farmacie* open in shopping hours and in turn for out of hours services; the address of the nearest open one is posted on all pharmacy doors.

INTERNET

Most good hotels will offer internet access (often charged) but a number of budget ones offer it free. The **Wi-fi access scheme** (www.veniceconnected.com) costs €8 per day; check the signal works in your chosen spots before buying a package. Partly given the above scheme, Venice has fewer **internet points** than desirable; useful ones are the toyshop on Campo Santa Barnaba and Net House Internet Café on Campo Santo Stefano. Costs are high, around €8 per hour.

L

LANGUAGE

Most Venetian hotels and shops will have staff who speak some English, French or German. However, in bars and cafés away from Piazza San Marco, you'll almost certainly have the chance to practise your Italian. For a **list of key phrases**, see the back cover of the pull-out map that comes with this book, or inside the back-cover flap.

Venetian Dialect

Venetians have a strong dialect, though to the visitor unfamiliar with the Italian language this is academic. However, do learn a bit as it's part of *Venexianarse,* becoming or feeling Venetian. Some terms are also useful to know: there is only one *piazza* in Venice – San Marco; other squares are usually called *campo,* although a small square may be known as a *piazzetta*; the term *calle* is used to refer to most streets, but a *salizzada* is a main street, and a covered passage is a *sottoportego.* A *ponte* is a bridge, a canal is a *rio,* and the broad paved walkway along a major waterfront or canal is a *riva* or a *fondamenta.*

Useful Venetian terms:

Ca' (from *casa*): house/palace
calle: alley
campo: square (plural *campi*)
campiello: small square
corte: external courtyard
cortile: internal courtyard
fontego or *fondaco:* historic warehouse
fondamenta: wide quayside
punta: a point
ramo: side street or dead end
rio (plural *rii*): curving canal lined by buildings
rio terrà: in-filled canal
riva: promenade, quayside
ruga: broad shopping street
rughetta: small shopping street
sacca: inlet
salizzada: main street; means 'paved'
sottoportico (or *sottoportego*): tiny alleyway running under a building
squero: boatyard
stazio: gondoliers' station

Notice that both Venetian and Italian names are used in street signs and on maps: for example, San Giuliano is 'San Zulian' and Santi Giovanni e Paolo is 'San Zanipolo' (Giovanni becomes 'Zani' in dialect).

M

MEDIA AND LISTINGS

Print Media

Newspapers and magazines *(giornali, riviste)*: you can find quality English-language newspapers at airports but in surprisingly few city-centre news-stands *(edicole),* mostly around San Marco, and always with a delay of 24 hours. For those who read Italian, the local newspaper is *Il Gazzettino.*

Listings Magazines

In Venice, the only reliable listings magazine is the bi-monthly *Shows & Events,* available from the city's tourist

offices (charge), which includes opening times for the month, and details of all major exhibitions and events.

Venice's other listings magazine is *Un Ospite di Venezia* (available online in English and Italian at www. unospitedivenezia.it). It is user-friendly and a useful additional source for listings, but the one detailed above is far better. Listed online are current attractions, concerts, events and exhibitions, including opening times and prices. It also has a useful section on practical information.

Television and Radio

The Italian state television network, RAI (Radio Televisione Italiana), broadcasts three main channels, which compete with multiple independent ones, which are mostly dire. All programmes are in Italian, including British and American feature films and imports, which are dubbed. Better hotels have cable connections for CNN Europe, CNBC and other channels that offer world news in English including BBC World and Sky. Most radio stations broadcast popular music. The BBC World Service can be picked up on shortwave.

MONEY

Currency. Italy's monetary unit is the euro (€), which is divided into 100 cents. Banknotes are available in denominations of 500, 200, 100, 50, 20, 10 and 5 euros. There are coins for 2 and 1 euro, and for 50, 20, 10, 5, 2 and 1 cents.

Currency Exchange. *Bureau de change* offices *(cambi)* usually open Monday to Friday, although hours do vary (Travelex offices at Piazza San Marco and the airport). Both *cambi* and banks charge a commission. Banks generally offer higher exchange rates and lower commissions. Passports are usually required when changing money.

ATMs. Automatic currency-exchange machines *(bancomat)* are operated by most banks and provide a convenient way of taking out money. Independent (non-bank related) ATMs can also be found in the centre of town.

Credit Cards and Traveller's Cheques. Most hotels, shops and restaurants take credit cards. If the card's sign is posted in the window of a business, they must accept it. Traveller's cheques are less readily acceptable, and you will usually get better value if you exchange them at a bank. Passports are needed when cashing traveller's cheques.

OPENING HOURS

Banks. Hours are Monday–Friday 8.30am–1.30pm, 2.35–3.30pm.

Bars and Restaurants. Some café-bars open for breakfast, but others do not open until around noon; the vast majority shut early, at around 10.30 or 11pm. Old-fashioned *bacari* (wine and tapas bars) in the Rialto area often

close early (at around 9.30pm). Most restaurants close at least one day a week; some close for parts of August, January and February.

Churches. The 16 Chorus Churches *(see p.100)* are open Mon–Sat 10am–5pm. The Frari is also open Sun 1–6pm. Other churches are normally open Mon–Sat from around 8am until noon and from 3 or 4pm–6 or 7pm. Sunday openings vary, some are only open for morning services.

Museums and Galleries. Some close one day a week (usually Monday), but otherwise open at 9 or 10am–6pm.

Shops. Open Monday to Saturday, 9 or 10am–1pm, and 3 or 4–7pm. Some shops open all day and even on Sunday, particularly in peak season.

P

POLICE

Although you rarely see them, Venice's police *(Polizia* or *Carabinieri)* function efficiently and are courteous. The emergency phone number is 112 or 113, which connects you to a switchboard and someone who speaks your language.

POST OFFICES

The most convenient post offices are on the Rialto at Calle San Salvador 5106, San Marco (Mon–Fri 8.30am–6pm), and at Lista di Spagna 233, Cannaregio, (Mon–Sat 8.30am–2pm). Postage

stamps *(francobolli)* are sold at post offices and tobacconists *(tabacchi),* marked by a distinctive 'T' sign.

PUBLIC HOLIDAYS

Banks, offices, most shops and museums close on public holidays *(giorni festivi)*. When a major holiday falls on a Thursday or a Tuesday, there may be a *ponte* (bridge) to the weekend, meaning Friday or Monday is taken, too.

The most important holidays are:

1 January	Capodanno/ Primo dell'Anno
6 January	Epifania
25 April	Festa della Liberazione
1 May	Festa del Lavoro (Labour Day)
15 August	Ferragosto (Assumption)
1 November	Ognissanti (All Saints)
8 December	Immacolata Concezione (Immaculate Conception)
25 December	Natale (Christmas Day)
26 December	Santo Stefano (Boxing Day)
Moveable	Pasquetta (Easter Monday)

The **Festa della Salute** (21 Nov) and the **Redentore** (third Sunday of July) are special Venetian holidays, when many shops close.

R

RELIGION

Although predominantly Roman Catholic, Venice has congregations of

Above from far left: San Marco Basilica mosaic; gilding at the Palazzo Ducale.

all the major religions *(see list below)*.

Anglican. Church of St George, Campo San Vio, Dorsoduro.

Evangelical Lutheran. Campo Santi Apostoli, Cannaregio.

Greek Orthodox. Ponte dei Greci, Castello.

Jewish Synagogue. Campo del Ghetto Vecchio 1149, Cannaregio (tel: 041-715 012 and 041-715 389)

Roman Catholic. Basilica San Marco. Masses in Italian; confession in several languages in the summer.

SMOKING

In 2005, smoking was banned in public enclosed spaces throughout Italy. Smokers can face a fine up to €275 for breaking this law.

TELEPHONES

The country code for Italy is 39, and the area code for Venice is 041. You must dial the '041' prefix even when making local calls within the city. Note that smaller bars and businesses increasingly only have mobile numbers.

Telephone Boxes. It is rare to find phone boxes as Italy has the highest proportion of mobile phone ownership in Europe. Ones that exist (Santa Lucia station and Piazzale Roma bus station) use phone cards *(schede telefoniche)* bought from Telecom offices.

Mobile Phones. EU mobile (cell) phones can be used in Italy, but check compatibility or buy an Italian SIM card, available from any mobile phone shop, if you are staying for long. Major networks are offered by Telecom Italia (TIM), Vodafone and Wind.

International Calls. Dial 00, followed by the country code (Australia +61, Ireland +353, New Zealand +64, South Africa +27, UK +44, US and Canada +1), then the area code (often minus the initial zero) then the number.

TIME ZONE

Italy is an hour ahead of Greenwich Mean Time (GMT). From the last Sunday in March to the last Sunday in October, clocks go forward an hour.

TIPPING

A service charge of 10 or 12 percent is often added to restaurant bills, so it is not necessary to tip much – perhaps just round up the bill. However, it is normal to tip porters, tour guides and elderly gondoliers who help you into and out of your craft at landing stations.

TOILETS

There are toilets *(toilette, gabinetti)*, usually of a reasonable standard but with a charge, at the airport, station, in car parks and some main squares. You can use the facilities in bars and cafés but only if you order a drink. *Signori* means men; *signore* means women.

TOURIST INFORMATION

The Italian National Tourist Board (ENIT) has an inadequate website so best to only trust the **Venice Tourist Board** site, which lists events, itineraries, excursions and hotels: www.turismovenezia.it. There's also a helpline for visitors: tel: 039 039 039. **ENIT** offices abroad may provide basic information:

Australia Level 4, 46 Market Street, Sydney; tel: 02-9262 1666.

Canada 175 Bloor Street East, Suite 907, South Tower, Toronto, Ontario M4W 3R8; tel: 416-925 3870; www.italiantourism.com.

UK/Ireland 1 Princes Street, London W1B 2AY; tel: 020-7399 3562; www.enit.it.

US

• **Chicago:** 500 N. Michigan Avenue, Suite 2240, Chicago, IL 60611; tel: 312-644 0996; www.italiantourism.com.

• **Los Angeles:** 12400 Wilshire Boulevard, Suite 550, Los Angeles CA 90025; tel: 310-820 0098; www.italiantourism.com.

• **New York:** 630 Fifth Avenue, Suite 1565, New York, NY 10111; tel: 212-245 4822; www.italiantourism.com.

Tourist Information Offices in Venice. The best tourist office (APT) is in the **Venice Pavilion** (tel: 041-529 8711) beside the Giardinetti Reali (Public Gardens). The hard-working but understaffed office is open daily 10am–6pm. There is an even busier office on the western corner of **Piazza** **San Marco**, opposite Museo Correr: San Marco 71/f, Calle dell'Ascensione/Procuratie Nuove; daily 9am–3.30pm. Both offices supply information, but most of it, even maps, events listings and other brochures, has to be paid for. They also offer booking for tours and events.

The tourist office at the railway station is also useful: **APT Venezia, Stazione Santa Lucia** (daily 8am–6.30pm), as is the one at the airport: **APT Marco Polo** (daily 9.30am–7.30pm). This mostly deals with accommodation and transport tickets.

Tourism Passes

To keep costs down, and avoid queuing, it's worth pre-booking museum, church and transport passes, especially for St Mark's Basilica, the Doge's Palace and the Accademia. Attractions that *must* be pre-booked are the Clock Tower and the Secret Itineraries tour of the Doge's Palace *(see p.101)*.

Venice Connected (www.veniceconnected.com) is an integrated, online-only booking system for 12 key museums and transport options, with discounts offered in quieter periods to encourage sustainable tourism.

Hello Venezia (www.hellovenezia.it; tel: 041-24 24) is most useful as a transport and/or museum-booking system and sells the **Venice Card,** which covers 12 museums and the 16 Chorus Churches *(see p.100)*, and offers the full range of integrated transport passes for different times.

Rolling Venice. A youth pass for those between 14 and 29. For €4, it provides

Above from far
left: Venice trans-
port old and new.

museum discounts, shopping, restaurant and hotel discounts, and a
discounted 72-hour vaporetto pass for
only €18. Sign up at the train station,
or the ACTV office in Piazzale Roma.
Vivaticket (www.vivaticket.it; tel: 84
808 2000, Italy-only call centre) is a
booking service for opera, concerts,
ballet and blockbuster exhibitions, as
well as major attractions and unusual
guided tours, notably the Secret Itineraries tour and the Clock Tower.

The Chorus Pass (www.chorus
venezia.org; tel: 041-275 0462) allows
access to 16 Venetian churches
(including the Frari), with charges
going towards local church restoration
projects *(see p.100).*

TRANSPORT

Getting to Venice

By Air: Companies flying from the
UK include British Airways
(www.britishairways.com) and EasyJet
(www.easyjet.com). Ryanair (www.
ryanair.com) runs flights from
Stansted to Treviso airport (32km/20
miles from Venice). Aer Lingus (tel:
0870 876 5000, www.flyaerlingus.
com) operate services from Dublin to
Venice. From the US there are direct
flights from New York (Delta Airlines,
www.delta.com) and other gateways
through Alitalia (www.alitalia.it).

By Train: Stazione Ferroviaria Santa
Lucia is well-connected to Turin, Milan,
Florence and Rome, as well as Paris and
London. Travel via Eurostar/Thello,
departing London 2.55pm and arriving

in Venice at 9.30am the following day,
or book a rail pass (International Rail,
tel: 0871 231 0790).
By Car: please see **Driving** section
(above) – but don't arrive by car unless
you really have to.

From the airport to Venice

Venice Marco Polo is Venice's main
airport, 13km (8 miles) north (tel: 041-
260 9260; www.veniceairport.it).

Public buses (ACTV) run from the
airport to the terminus at Piazzale
Roma every half-hour in summer and
once an hour in winter; airport buses
(ATVO) have a similar timetable,
journey time (30 minutes) and price
(€5 single). Buy tickets from ATVO
office in the arrivals terminal. Once
at Piazzale Roma, board the No. 1
vaporetto for an all-stages ride along
the Grand Canal; take the No. 2 if you
want the quickest route to San Marco.
The new Ponte Calatrava also connects by foot to the main train station.

Public water launches: Alilaguna
(www.alilaguna.it) connects Venice
and the airport (€25 return); key routes
are Blue (Blu) to Fondamente Nuove
(45 minutes) and Orange (Arancio)
to San Marco (90 minutes).

Private water taxis *(taxi acquei)*: the
speediest and most stylish way to arrive
(30 minutes) but the priciest (from
€100), so don't confuse them with the
Alilaguna craft. Taxis will take you to
your hotel if it has a water entrance.
For all water transport from the airport
you have to walk about 500m/yds from
the new terminal to the small docks.

Treviso is a small airport 32km (20 miles) north of Venice, used mainly by charters and low-cost airlines such as Ryanair, who, confusingly, call it 'Venice airport'. ATVO's Eurobus runs between Treviso and Piazzale Roma.

Getting around Venice

A water **transport map** (€3) is available from all Venice tourist offices, and Hello Venezia offices (including on Piazzale Roma (tel. 041-24 24, www.hellovenezia.it). Check ferry routes on the public ACTV water transport site (www.actv.it), which is reliable for maps, timetables and ferry routes for the vaporetti (waterbuses):

Venice Connected deals with integrated transport, including pre-booking transport and museum passes and offers a good interactive map.

Pre-book a city transport pass (including islands), which is good value: €50 for 7 days, €35 for 3 days, €30 for 2 days, €25 for 36 hours, €20 for 24 hours; €18 for 12 hours; €7 for an hour's journey (discounted on www. veniceconnected.com). Before every journey, swipe the pass by holding the rechargeable electronic card up to the sensor by the boarding pier: a green light and a bleep means the pass is valid; otherwise seek assistance.

Vaporetti (waterbuses)

These workhorses will take you to within a short walk of anywhere you want to visit. The main waterbus services are: **No. 1**, which stops at every landing stage along the Grand Canal; **No. 2**, provides a faster service down the Grand Canal as part of its circular San Marco, Giudecca canal, Piazzale Roma route (and the Lido). **Nos 41** (anticlockwise) and **42** (clockwise) take a circular route, calling at San Zaccaria, Il Redentore, Piazzale Roma, the railway station, Fondamente Nuove, San Michele, Murano and Sant'Elena. Vaporetti **Nos 51** and **52** also provide long, scenic, circular tours around the periphery, as well as stopping at Murano; in summer they go on to the Lido (change at Fondamente Nuove to do the whole route). Note that the circular routes travel up the Cannaregio canal, stopping at Guglie, and then skirting the northern shores of Venice. **Nos 61** and **62** provide a fast route between Piazzale Roma and the Lido, going via the Zattere (Giudecca canal). For Burano, take the **LN (Laguna Nord)** line from Fondamente Nuove via Murano. **Line T** connects Burano with Torcello.

Gondolas: The official daytime rate is €80 for 40 minutes (up to six people), then €40–50 for each subsequent 20 minutes. The evening rate (from 8pm–8am) is €100.

Water Taxis (motoscafi): a door-to-door service that comes at a high cost.

Traghetti. The traghetto (gondola ferry, 50 cents) operates at key points across the Grand Canal. It is customary (but not obligatory) to stand while crossing.

Art Vaporetto: This new art heritage water line travels between key museums and the daily cost (€24) can be partly offset against the transport pass if booked with that pass (Vaporetto dell'arte, www.vaporettoarte.com, tel. 041-24 24).

Walking: Venice is so compact that it is often quicker (and cheaper) to walk than to hop on a water bus. Enjoy getting lost on foot: official addresses are confusing; always ask for the name of the nearest church or square *(campo).*

WEBSITES

A round-up of online sites, all mentioned earlier, that will help you plan your trip:

Transport and Museums:
ACTV (www.actv.it): Public water transport: maps, routes and timetables.
HelloVenezia (www.hellovenezia.it) for booking integrated transport, ticketing and museums.
Venice Connected (www.veniceconnected.com) for integrated transport, ticketing and museums, including pre-booking transport and museum passes. Also a good interactive map of Venice: **ASM transport** (www.asmvenezia.it).

Culture and Events:
Venice tourist board (www.turismovenezia.it) for what's on in Venice: events, itineraries, excursions, hotels.
La Biennale (www.labiennale.org)

Venice's arts jamboree, in uneven years, **Venetian Club (**www.thevenetianclub.co.uk) crafts, cookery and Venetian-style rowing courses.

Exploring and Background:
Venice in Peril (www.veniceinperil.org): avoid its advice at your peril.
Salve (www.salve.it): Saving Venice, including the MOSE mobile barrier, and excursions to see it.
Vivere Venezia (www.viverevenezia.com): helpful advice on visiting or living in Venice.
Tap Venice Eating: iPhone app from iTunes (£1.79). Reliable insiders' restaurant guide by local, Michela Scibilia, and tagged by 'best seafood' 'scenic view', etc.

WOMEN

Venice is an extremely safe city and arguably there is far less hassling and unwanted attention than anywhere else in Italy. Even late at night, catching ferries, or walking around Central Venice alone, Venice feels astonishingly unthreatening.

YOUTH HOSTELS

There are half a dozen youth hostels *(ostelli della gioventù)* in Venice, with three in Giudecca, the best location. Particularly recommended is **Ostello Venezia** (Fondamenta delle Zitelle, Giudecca 86; tel: 041-523 8211; www.hostelvenice.org).

Above from far left: Venetian flag; sculptures on the south side of the Basilica San Marco.

Venice excels at cultural one-upmanship. You can sleep in Tchaikovsky's bed or wake up in palaces that welcomed doges, Henry James and Hemingway. If you hanker after decadence and drama, choose a grand pile on the Grand Canal. If you yearn for a quiet life, chiming bells and secret gardens, slip into a family-owned *palazzo* in the backwaters of Cannaregio. Or, for a sense of Venice before the interior decorators moved in, retreat to a bucolic inn in Burano, the lagoon's friendliest island.

Venice is over-burdened with palatial piles, but there is now great choice at the more modest end, from boutique retreats to chic guesthouses, eclectic B&Bs, Gothic apartments, or intimate, family-owned *palazzi*.

The lack of standardisation cuts both ways: each room is delightfully different but, on the other hand, even in a distinguished hotel, the rooms at the front may be glorious, but hide dingy garrets at the back.

Apartments: A delightful way of experiencing the city, even revelling in a Gothic *palazzo* complete with gondola dock. **Venetian Apartments** (UK tel: 020 3356 9667; www.venice-rentals.com) are the market leaders, with a reliable range of fully-vetted apartments to suit couples, families or even celebratory house-parties.

B&Bs: This is an effective way of getting to meet local people. For a wide range of B&Bs, see BB Planet (www.bbplanet.com) and check by district and price; also see the Venice tourist board website (www.turismovenezia.it).

Outside Central Venice: Apart from Giudecca, consider the islands of Burano, Murano and the Lido. If staying outside the city, avoid soulless Mestre and opt for Padua or Treviso, a 30-minute train ride from Venice.

San Marco

Albergo Hotel San Samuele
Salizzada San Samuele; tel: 041-520 5165; vaporetto: San Samuele. €

Tucked away behind Palazzo Grassi, this central, renovated budget hotel has charming service, provided by a hands-on owner, sunny, pared-down rooms and free Wi-fi. It's great value for this arty area

Flora
Calle dei Bergamaschi, off Calle Larga XXII Marzo; tel: 041-520 5844; www.hotelflora.it; vaporetto: Santa Maria del Giglio; €€€

A sought-after family-run hotel in a quiet spot near St Mark's. Rooms can be palatial or poky (No. 32 leads to the garden). Breakfast in secluded courtyard garden; gym; massage; tearoom.

Gritti Palace
Campo Santa Maria del Giglio; tel: 041-296 1222; www.hotelgrittipalace

---

Price for a double room for one night without breakfast:

€€€€   over 400 euros
€€€   280–400 euros
€€   140–280 euros
€   below 140 euros

venice.com; vaporetto: Santa Maria del Giglio; €€€€

Hemingway, Churchill and Greta Garbo all stayed in this 15th-century palace. The most patrician hotel in Venice, it retains the air of a private *palazzo*, with Murano chandeliers and damask furnishings. Reopens after major refurbishment in spring 2013.

Locanda Orseolo

Corte Zorzi, San Marco 1083, tel: 041-520 4827; vaporetto San Marco. €€

A friendly, family-run hotel with exceptionally helpful staff close to St Mark's. Cosy, traditional, Venetian-style rooms overlook canal or courtyard.

Locanda Novecento

Calle del Dose; tel: 041-241 3765; www.locanda novecento.biz; vaporetto: Santa Maria del Giglio; €€

This ethnic-chic boutique hotel offers an exotic touch of Marrakesh, with funky Moroccan lamps and Turkish rugs. There are beamed ceilings, cosy bedrooms and a tiny courtyard for breakfast.

Luna Baglioni

Calle Larga dell' Ascensione; tel: 041-528 9840; www.baglionihotels. com; vaporetto: San Marco-Vallaresso; €€€€

The oldest hotel in Venice, this was originally a Knights Templar lodge for pilgrims en route to Jerusalem. Just off Piazza San Marco, it has Venetian decor, an 18th-century ballroom and the grandest breakfast room in Venice.

Monaco e Grand

Calle Vallaresso; tel: 041-520 0211; www.hotel monaco.it; vaporetto: San Marco-Vallaresso; €€€-€€€€

A mix of slick contemporary and classic Venetian style, with a chic bar and waterfront breakfast room. The Palazzo Salvadego annexe is more typically Venetian, and less expensive (€€€), but shares the same smart breakfast room.

Castello

Casa Querini

Campo San Giovanni Novo; tel: 041-241 1294; www.locandaquerini.com; vaporetto: San Zaccaria or Rialto; €€

A small inn close to Campo Santa Maria Formosa. Eleven spacious, low-key rooms, decorated in 17th-century Venetian style. Pleasant staff.

Danieli

Riva degli Schiavoni; tel: 041-522 6480; www. starwoodhotels.com/danieli; vaporetto: San Zaccaria; €€€€

Set on the waterfront, this world-famous hotel has a splendid Gothic foyer, and plush rooms with parquet floors and gilded bedsteads. Choose the *casa vecchia* doge's residence not the 'Danielino' luxe part. Splendid rooftop bar and restaurant, La Terrazza.

Liassidi Palace

Ponte dei Greci; tel: 041-520 5658; www.liassidipalacehotel.com; vaporetto: San Zaccaria; €€€

A boutique hotel in a Gothic palace behind the Riva degli Schiavoni with a

muted yet sleek interior. The individualistic bedrooms range from Art Deco to Bauhaus. Bar but no restaurant.

Locanda La Corte

Calle Bressana; tel: 041-241 1300; www.locandalacorte.it; vaporetto: Ospedale; €–€€

Small Gothic palace off Campo SS Giovanni e Paolo. The decor is a muted version of the traditional Venetian style. There's an inner courtyard for breakfast. Bedrooms overlook the canal or the courtyard.

Londra Palace

Riva degli Schiavoni; tel: 041-520 0533; www.londrapalace.com; vaporetto: San Zaccaria; €€€–€€€€

Londra Palace, where Tchaikovsky composed his Fourth Symphony, is a grande dame, with 100 windows overlooking the lagoon. A room with a view will transform your stay. For drama and waterside bustle, get a fourth-floor room overlooking the lagoon. Or hide out under the eaves on the fifth floor, where 502 has views across the lagoon to San Giorgio.

Metropole

Riva degli Schiavoni; tel: 041-520 5044; www.hotelmetropole.com; vaporetto: San Zaccaria; €€€€

This boutique hotel is dotted with eclectic antiques and objets d'art. It has a Michelin-starred restaurant called Met, a trendy bar, lovely garden courtyard and lagoon or canal views; rooms can be cosy (No. 350) or amusingly kitsch (No. 251).

Palazzo Schiavoni

Fondamenta dei Furlani; tel: 041-241 1275; www. palazzoschiavoni.com; vaporetto: San Zaccaria; €€

Rooms and apartments in a tasteful conversion (with the odd frescoed ceiling) beside the Scuola di San Giorgio. A good choice for families.

Dorsoduro

Accademia Villa Marevege

Fondamenta Bollani; tel: 041-521 0188; www. pensioneaccademia.it; vaporetto: Accademia; €€

Gracious, highly sought-after wisteria-clad villa at the Grand Canal end of Rio San Trovaso. Atmospheric bedrooms and lovely canalside gardens, where breakfast is served in summer, and sunsets are toasted in style.

Bloom/7 Cielo

Campiello Santo Stefano 3470, tel: (+39) 340 149 8872; www.settimocielo-venice.com; vaporetto: Accademia; €€

Overlooking Campo Santo Stefano, these twin B&Bs are set on the upper floors of a grand *palazzo* but are different in mood. **7 Cielo** (Seventh Heaven) is overtly romantic, with Murano-tiled bathrooms and moody bedrooms. **Bloom** is distinctly Baroque, with bold colours and gilded beds.

Ca' Maria Adele

Rio Terrà Catecumeni; tel: 041-520 3078; www. camariaadele.it; vaporetto: Salute; €€€–€€€€

Baroque glamour, bohemian charm and canalside views in a boutique gem

beside La Salute. The Doge's Room is a riot of red brocade; the Sala dei Mori, has lovely views. Attentive staff.

Ca' Pisani

Rio Terrà Foscarini; tel: 041-240 1411; www.capisanihotel.it; vaporetto: Accademia or Zattere; €€–€€€

In a historic *palazzo* near the Accademia, this is a glamorous, Art Deco-style retreat, rather retro despite Wi-fi throughout. Other touches include peaceful patio breakfasts, and the hip wine bar/restaurant.

Ca' San Trovaso

Fondamenta delle Eremite; tel: 041-277 1146; www.casantrovaso.com; vaporetto: Ca' Rezzonico or San Basilio; €

Unpretentious little hotel on a quiet canal has terracotta floors and damask wallpaper, but no TV or phones in rooms. Nice roof terrace.

Charming House DD.724

Ramo de Mula 724; tel: 041-277 0262; www.thecharminghouse.com; vaporetto: Accademia; €€€

This sleek, modernist-chic designer retreat is quirky and cosy enough to appeal to old Venetian hands. Consider DD.694, the sister apartment nearby, and a similar retreat in Castello.

Don Orione

Rio Tera Foscarini; tel: 041-522 4077; vaporetto: Accademia; €

On a square near the Accademia, this former orphanage and monastery is now a superior hostel run by a religious foundation. Gardens and Gothic cloisters open to guests. Comfortable rooms, private bathrooms; restaurant.

Locanda Art Deco

Calle delle Botteghe; tel: 041-277 0558; www.locandaartdeco.com; vaporetto: Sant'Angelo or Accademia; €€

Near the Accademia, it is matched by the Residenza, its sister apartments, which were good enough for Angelina Jolie's entourage. Both get the services of Alex Hai, the female gondolier.

Locanda San Barnaba

Calle del Traghetto; tel: 041-241 1233; vaporetto: Ca' Rezzonico; €–€€

This small inn near Ca' Rezzonico occupies a 16th-century frescoed palace run by the ancestral owner. Venetian-style rooms, a few with balconies, and a pretty canalside courtyard for breakfast.

La Calcina

Fondamenta Zattere ai Gesuati; tel: 041-520 6466; www.lacalcina.com; vaporetto: Zattere; €€

Overlooking Giudecca canal, this romantic inn is where John Ruskin lodged in 1876. Lovely roof terrace, nice bedrooms, waterside La Piscina dining room and terrace. Book early.

Cannaregio, San Polo and Santa Croce

Abbazia

Calle Priuli dei Cavaletti; tel: 041-717 333; www.abbaziahotel.com; vaporetto: Ferrovia; €€

Above from far left: terrace with unbeatable views at the Luna Baglioni *(see p.111)*; Hotel Danieli reception *(see p.111)*; the delightful Ca' Pisani.

Set close to the Ca' d'Oro, this romantic 16th-century palace features stuccoed salons adorned with School of Tintoretto paintings and Murano chandeliers, matched by frescoed, silk-lined bedrooms and sumptuous beds. Canalside views and a secret garden.

Domus Orsoni

Corte Vedei; tel: 041-275 9538; www.domusorsoni.it; vaporetto: San Marcuola; €–€€

Set near the Ghetto, this stylish, mosaic-studded guesthouse belongs to a mosaic-producing company with the only furnace allowed to function in central Venice; attractive walled garden; try a mosaic course too.

Ca' Sagredo

Campo Santa Sofia; tel: 041-241 3111; www. casagredohotel.com; vaporetto: Ca' d'Oro; €€€–€€€€

Ca' Sagredo occupies an historic Grand Canal *palazzo* adorned with fabulous frescoes by Tiepolo and Sebastiano Ricci. Many rooms have Grand Canal views; breakfast under a Tiepolo ceiling; sip cocktails at the canalside bar. Can provide a babysitter, personal shopper or personal trainer.

Casa del Melograno

Campiello del Ponte Storto; tel: 041-520 8807; www.locanda delmelograno.it; vaporetto: San Marcuola; €

Tucked off busy Strada Nuova shopping street, this is a great budget option, with a garden, and rooms remodelled in a simple modern style.

Giorgione

Santi Apostoli; tel: 041-522 5810; www.hotelgiorgione.com; vaporetto: Ca' d'Oro; €€

Not far from the Ca' d'Oro, this family-run, 15th-century *palazzo* offers appealing balconies. Decor is traditional Venetian, with chandeliers and Murano glass; the breakfast room opens onto a courtyard; free afternoon coffee and cakes.

Grand Hotel Dei Dogi

Fondamenta Madonna dell'Orto; tel: 041-220 8111; www.boscolohotels.com; €€€–€€€€; vaporetto: Madonna dell'Orto

Luxury hotel on the edge of the lagoon. A former monastery, it is an oasis of calm, with tasteful Venetian decor and the largest, loveliest hotel garden in Venice; courtesy motorboat.

Ai Mori d'Oriente

Fondamenta della Sensa; tel: 041-711 001; www. morihotel.com; vaporetto: Madonna dell'Orto; €€–€€€

Quirky boutique hotel near the Ghetto with lots of character and eclectic and exotic touches, plus welcoming staff.

749 Ponte Chiodo

Ponte Chiodo; tel: 041-241 3935; www.ponte chiodo.it; vaporetto: Ca' d'Oro; €

In a quiet area of Cannaregio, this is a budget guesthouse with rare amenities such as Wi-fi and air conditioning. Friendly owner provides valuable information about the city.

Islands: The Giudecca

Bauer Palladio Hotel & Spa

Fondamenta della Croce, Isola della Giudecca; tel: 041-520 7022; www.bauervenezia.com; vaporetto: Zitelle; €€€–€€€€

Set in Palladio-designed cloisters, this serene, somewhat austere space has garden terraces, canalside views and a special spa; courtesy shuttle boat to the more worldly Bauers over the water. Closed mid-Nov–mid-March.

Casa Genoveffa

Calle del Forno, Giudecca 472; tel: (+39) 347 250 7809; www.casagenoveffa.com; vaporetto: Palanca. €–€€

Tucked away down a back alley, this unpretentious but cosy B&B has beamed rooms and four-poster beds.

Cipriani

Isola della Giudecca 10; tel: 041-520 7744; www. hotelcipriani.com; vaporetto: Zitelle; €€€€

The Cipriani can be seen as a cliché, but it conveys a sense of warmth and intimacy better than most grand hotels.

Hilton Molino Stucky

Isola della Giudecca 753; tel: 041-272 3311; www. molinostucky hilton.com; vaporetto: Palanca; €€€

This formidable-looking flour mill on the Giudecca waterfront is a luxury hotel with a rooftop pool, magical terrace and the cool Skybar lounge. There's a spa, several restaurants, a ground-floor bar and a shuttle boat to St Mark's.

Islands: the Lido, Murano, Burano and Torcello

Locanda Cipriani

Piazza Santa Fosca, Isola di Torcello; tel: 041-730 0150; www.locandacipriani.com; €€

Bucolic inn beloved by Hemingway and set in a remote spot. Run by a branch of the Cipriani family, it has a celebrated restaurant, with a garden for outdoor dining. Closed Jan and Tues.

Murano Palace

Fondamenta Vetrai 77, Isola di Murano; tel: 041-739 655; www.muranopalace.com; ferry: Colonna; €–€€

A rewarding, under-priced gem, with splendid Murano chandeliers and canal views. Enjoy sailing, rowing and fishing, and the family's restaurant nearby.

Rivamare

Lungomare Marconi 44, Lido; tel: 041-5260352; www.hotelrivamare. com; vaporetto: Lido; €–€€

A welcoming, family-run beach hotel, perfect for families. Some rooms have sea views and small balconies and there's a terrace. There is a separately-run meditation and Reiki centre.

Venissa

Fondamenta Santa Caterina, Isola di Mazzorbo (Burano); tel: 041-527 2281; www.venissa.it; vaporetto: Mazzorbo 41/42; €€

Run by the Bisol prosecco dynasty, this quaint guesthouse, gourmet restaurant and wine estate revels in creative cuisine *(see Tour 12)*.

Above from far left: grand staircase; lavish room at the Cipriani.

RESTAURANTS

Venetian restaurants range in style from cool, 18th-century elegance – especially in San Marco and Castello – to rustic gentility. Yet individualistic inns abound, tucked under pergolas or spilling onto terraces and court-yards. More up-market places are termed *ristoranti*, but may be called *osterie* (inns) if they focus on homely food in an intimate or rustic setting. Restaurants covered in the Tours are not listed here. *Bacari* are traditional wine bars that also serve food, a Venetian version of tapas, known as *cicchetti*. Many *bacari* feature in the tours as they are an intrinsic part of Venetian life,

San Marco

Dining in the San Marco area can be tricky as overpriced tourist traps, grand cafés, and expensive established restaurants predominate. But moving away from St Mark's generally sees both the crowds (and the prices) fall away.

Acqua Pazza

Campo Sant'Angelo, San Marco 3808; tel: 041-277 0688; closed Mon; vaporetto: S. Angelo; €€–€€€

This slick, up-market spot on a trendy square is the place for huge pizzas (€€) or fine seafood (€€€).

> Price guide for a two-course meal for one with a glass of house wine:
>
> €€€€   over €85
> €€€   €55–85
> €€   €25–55
> €   up to €25

Caffè Centrale

Piscina Frezzeria, San Marco 1659b; tel: 041-887 6642; daily 7pm–2am; vaporetto: San Marco Vallaresso; €€€

This sleek lounge bar, late-night restaurant and music club in a converted cinema mixes modish cuisine and cutting-edge design and comes with gondola attached.

Cavatappi

Campo della Guerra, near San Zulian, San Marco 525; tel: 041-296 0252; closed Sun D and Mon; vaporetto: San Zaccaria or Rialto; €–€€.

A fashionable, contemporary-style wine bar serving *cicchetti*, light lunches and evening meals; trust the specials and the wines.

Enoteca Al Volto

Calle Cavalli 4081; tel: 041-522 8945; until 10pm, closed Sun; cash only; vaporetto: Rialto; €–€€

This is the place for wine by the glass accompanied by *cicchetti* or a more substantial bowl of pasta. The outdoor tables are soon snapped up but the back room is cosy, with a nautical feel.

Harry's Bar

Calle Vallaresso, San Marco 1323; tel: 041-528 5777; vaporetto: San Marco Vallaresso; €€€€

This legendary bar and restaurant is consistently good and draws a Venetian crowd. The unpretentious tone is perfect, set by the current Arrigo (Harry) Cipriani. Sip a Bellini (prosecco and peach juice, invented here), even if the price puts you off having a second.

PG's Restaurant

Palazzina Grassi, San Marco 3247; tel: 041-528 4644; daily; vaporetto: San Samuele. €€€€

Set in a Philippe Starck-designed boutique hotel halfway down the Grand Canal, this seductive gastro temple appeals to the art and film crowd. Chef Luigi Frascella combines Japanese and Italian styles: expect raw fish with yellow tiger-stripe, inky cuttlefish, or ravioli with walnut and ricotta.

Trattoria Do Forni

Calle degli Specchieri; tel: 041-523 2148; ; vaporetto: San Marco Giardinetti; €€€

An up-market but old-school spot. Reliable food in rambling yet intimate rooms, with atmosphere but no waterfront views. Italian classics along with international and Venetian dishes.

Castello

Castello offers a mixture of authentic inns and grandstanding luxury hotels, with sophisticated restaurants to match (see the **Accommodation** entries for luxury hotels that have noted restaurants). But hidden in alleys away from Riva degli Schiavoni are some more traditional inns.

Alle Testiere

Calle del Mondo Novo, Castello 5801; tel: 041-522 7220; closed Sun and Mon; vaporetto: Rialto or San Zaccaria; €€€

Near Campo Santa Maria Formosa, this renowned seafood restaurant demands booking (few tables). The menu recalls Venice's days on the Oriental spice route; razor clams or pasta may be subtly spiced; fine wine list.

Enoteca Mascareta

Calle Lunga Santa Maria Formosa; tel: 041-523 0744; open D only (7pm–2am); vaporetto: Rialto; €€

A cosy, rustic wine bar run by convivial wine writer Mauro Lorenzon. Nibble on *charcuterie* at the counter, or choose from the small menu. The eccentric host, laid-back jazz and superb wines ensure a contented Venetian clientele.

Il Covo

Campiello della Pescaria; tel 041-522 3812; closed Wed and Thur; vaporetto: Arsenale; €€€

Covo's fine reputation draws foodies to sample the fish-heavy tasting menu. The *moeche* (softshell crab) lightly fried with onions vie with Adriatic tuna, or squid-ink pasta with clams and courgette flowers. Booking is essential.

La Corte Sconta

Calle del Pestrin; tel: 041-522 7024; closed Sun and Mon; vaporetto: Arsenale; €€€

A renowned and authentic seafood spot, tucked in a secret courtyard, with a cheerful atmosphere and a menu based on fish fresh from Chioggia market. Tuck into fishy *antipasti*, from scallops to sardines. Book.

L'Osteria di Santa Marina

Campo Santa Marina; tel: 041-528 5239; closed Sun, and Mon L; vaporetto: Rialto; €€€

Above from far left: al fresco lunch; the cheese tray.

Opening Times
Where no times are given in these listings, restaurants are open daily for lunch and dinner.

Reservations
Always book in advance for fancier restaurants, and, because local people (especially at weekends) flock to high-quality, but reasonably priced, eateries, reservations are advisable in general. Normally a call the day before or the morning of the meal will do the trick, but to avoid disappointment at weekends, book a few days ahead.

Vegetarians in Venice

It can be challenging for non fish-eaters but appeal to the creativity of the chef; also try La Zucca, Tearoom Caffè Orientale and *bacari* such as Fiore, Alla Vedova and Oniga, as well as Ca' Giustinian (big salads) and Acqua Pazza (pizza).

Cicchetti

Cicchetti (pronounced chi-kettee) are Venetian tapas. They're cheap but can be sensational, from *calamari* and meatballs, to marinated radicchio, fried mozzarella balls, Venetian sushi, shrimp wrapped in pancetta, asparagus tarts, or *crostini* slathered with *baccalà* (salt cod).

Set in a quiet square, this deceptively simple trattoria presents reinterpretations of Venetian classics, from cuttlefish-ink ravioli with sea bass to fresh turbot, beef carpaccio or tuna and bean soup. In summer, sit outside and finish with a cinnamon apple pie.

Dorsoduro

Dorsoduro, the smartest residential district in town, also represents chic dining. But, off the beaten track, the district is equally well-known for its low-key cafés, tucked away in the pretty backwaters.

Avogaria

Calle del'Avogaria 1629; tel: 041-296 0491; closed Mon and Tue; vaporetto: San Basilio; €€

With exposed brickwork, cool clientele and creative *cicchetti*, Avogaria is more than a modish tapas bar. After a few slivers of fishy delights, you might find yourself settling in for the risotto.

Cantinone già Schiavi

Fondamenta Nani, Rio di San Trovaso; tel: 041-523 0034; closes 9.30pm and Sun D; vaporetto: Zattere; €

This old-fashioned canalside wine bar is popular with Venetians and visitors alike. It's a good place for *cicchetti* – among the most inventive in Venice. Prop up the bar over a light lunch or linger over canalside cocktails (7–8pm).

Oniga

Campo San Barnaba; tel: 041-522 4410; closed Tue; vaporetto: Ca' Rezzonico; €€

Eat inside or on the campo, opting for the seafood platter or the vegetarian option. Vegetarians can be spoilt with pasta dishes made with artichokes, aubergines and pecorino cheese.

The Giudecca

The Giudecca represents one of Venice's most exciting dining areas, with authentic inns interspersed with formal dining in grande-dame hotels, notably the Cipriani. And the inns are often more authentic and better value than those along the waterfront around San Marco.

Alla Palanca

Fondamenta al Ponte Piccolo, Giudecca 448; tel: 041-528 7719; Mon–Sat L only; vaporetto: Palanca; €€

This neighbourhood bar-trattoria serves a short lunch-time menu. Grab one of the outdoor tables and observe the comings and goings over a plate of risotto in cuttlefish ink.

Altanella

Calle delle Erbe; tel: 041-522 7780; closed Mon and Tue; no credit cards; vaporetto: Palanca or Redentore; €€€

Friendly trattoria. Only fish dishes on offer, but afterwards try ice cream with grappa-soaked raisins. Lovely outdoor seating with sweeping views across the Guidecca Canal.

Do Mori

Fondamenta Sant'Eufemia; tel: 041-522 5452; closed Sun; vaporetto: Sant'Eufemia; €€

Formed by a breakaway group from Harry's Bar, this is the place for those who can't afford the elevated prices of the original. The food is sound Venetian home cooking, with a preponderance of fish dishes (good scampi risotto) plus pasta and pizzas.

Fortuny Restaurant

Hotel Cipriani, Fondamenta San Giovanni; tel: 041-520 7744; closed Nov–Mar; vaporetto: Zitelle; €€€–€€€€

The Fortuny spills onto a glorious terrace: the setting is exquisite, the formal service divine and the prices deadly. Or try the more informal (and relatively less pricey) **Cip's Club**. Both offer views across to San Marco and free launch service from St Mark's pier. Book ahead.

Harry's Dolci

Fondamenta San Biagio; tel: 041-522 4844; closed Tue and Nov–Feb; vaporetto: Sant' Eufemia; €€€

Come here for a waterside American brunch; it's Harry's without the hype, and with better views and prices. Try the Venetian risotto, come for cakes *(dolci)* outside meal times, or sip a signature Bellini in the bar.

San Polo, Santa Croce and Rialto

This area abounds in *bacari*, as well as in individualistic Rialto market inns that have a fiercely loyal local clientele.

Alla Madonna

Calle della Madonna; tel: 041-522 3824; closed Wed; vaporetto: Rialto Mercato; €€–€€€

This bustling, ever-popular trattoria serves meticulously prepared seafood. Tuck into Sant'Erasmo artichokes or a seafood risotto and be seduced by the impressive art collection (no bookings).

Alla Zucca

Ponte del Megio, off Campo San Giacomo del'Orio; tel: 041-524 1570; closed Sun and Aug; vaporetto: San Stae; €€

This popular trattoria is set by a crooked canal bridge, with a few tables outside. The bohemian atmosphere reflects the vegetable-inspired menu (aubergine pasta, smoked ricotta, pumpkin flan) as well as meat and fish. Book.

Al Nono Risorto

Sottoportego della Siora Bettina, Campo San Cassiano; tel: 041-524 1169; closed all day Wed and Thur L; vaporetto: San Silvestro; €€

A rustic spot, framed by a wisteria-hung courtyard and garden. With its radical-chic mood, it is particularly popular with thirty-something Venetians. Try the squid with polenta.

Al Vecio Fritolin

Calle della Regina; tel: 041-522 2881; closed Mon; vaporetto: San Stae; €€–€€€

Irina's cosy, quirky fish restaurant near the Rialto Bridge is the place for a seafood extravaganza, but it can also be the scene of a more modest pasta lunch. The full menu features mixed fried fish, soft-shell crab and swordfish tartare.

Above from far left: carpaccio; lunch by the canal; pasta and fresh pesto, with a sprinkling of pine nuts and parmesan – the simpler the better.

Meal Times
Most restaurants close between lunch and dinner sittings. Lunch is normally served between 12.30pm and 2.30pm, with dinner service starting around 7pm. Try to adjust to the local time in order to take the best advantage of the menu (go too late, and they may run out of things!). Late-night dining can be difficult to find, so you will generally need to settle on somewhere by 9pm.

Cantina Do Spade

Calle delle Do Spade, Rialto; tel: 041-521 0583; closed Sun; vaporetto: Rialto Mercato; €

One of the oldest Rialto *bacari*, still going strong, run by a friendly young team keen to tempt you with deep-fried *calamari*, *baccalà* (salt cod), meatballs and other typical Venetian *cicchetti*. Stand at the bar or grab a table for a traditional meal.

Da Fiore

Calle del Scaleter, off Campo di San Polo; tel: 041-721 308; closed Sun and Mon; vaporetto: S. Tomà; €€€€

Regularly dubbed the best restaurant in town, this is a celebrity haunt during the Film Festival. At best, Da Fiore reflects the subtlety of Venetian cuisine, from grilled *calamari* and *granseola* (spider crab) to Adriatic tuna, sashimi and *risotto al nero di seppia* (cuttlefish risotto). Only one (much sought-after) table overlooks the canal.

Ristorante Ribot

Fondamenta Minotto, Rio del Gaffaro, Santa Croce; tel: 041-524 2486; closed Sun; €€

This authentic neighbourhood restaurant is superb value (try the risotto, grilled scallops or seafood pasta) but also has a secret garden, and in the evening, a warm atmosphere, thanks to the live music and friendly service.

Tearoom Caffè Orientale

Rio Marin, Santa Croce 888; tel: 041-520 1789; noon–9pm, closed Thur; vaporetto: Riva de Biasio; €

This is an arty tearoom serving cakes and pastries. It also does light vegetarian fare, such as asparagus or artichoke quiches, a rarity for Venice

Cannaregio

Cannaregio has a great number of everyday inns – the area is studded with typical *bacari*. The ones around Strada Nuova are lively by day, those around Fondamenta della Misericordia come alive by night.

Al Fontego dei Pescatori

Calle Priuli; tel: 041-520 0538; closed Mon; vaporetto: Ca' d'Oro; €€

Lolo, the owner, is president of the Rialto fish market and has his own stall, so the fish is always wonderfully fresh, and matched by fine Veneto and Friuli wines. The wide selection of seafood includes an elegantly presented platter of raw fish, grilled cuttlefish served with white polenta, scallops and sea bass.

Algiubagio

Fondamente Nuove 5039; tel: 041-523 6084; closed Tue; vaporetto: Fondamente Nuove; €–€€

This contemporary *bacaro* is the perfect place for *cicchetti* while waiting for the ferry to the islands. The creative (but pricier) restaurant is popular with local people.

Alla Frasca

Campiello della Carità; tel: 041-528 5433; closed Tue; vaporetto: Fondamente Nuove; €

Hidden in the backstreets, this friendly, neighbourhood inn serves fresh, no-

frills food at decent prices; eat grilled fish or spaghetti with clams in the pretty courtyard and feel like a Venetian.

Al Vecio Bragozzo

Strada Nuova, Cannaregio 4386; tel: 041-523 7277; closed Mon; vaporetto: Ca' d'Oro; €€

It can be hard to distinguish among the tourist places that lie along the Strada Nuova, but this restaurant caters to both locals and tourists. The owner's brother has a fishing *bragozzo*, which hauls in fresh seafood each day. Try the classically Venetian *sardèle in soar* (Venetian sardines in an onion sauce with pine nuts and raisins).

Anice Stellato

Fondamenta della Sensa; tel: 041-720 744; closed Mon–Tue; vaporetto: Guglie or Sant'Alvise; €€

This small, family-run restaurant is a long way from the centre but always busy (book if you can). Come for the *cicchetti* or for a full meal, including pasta with prawns and courgette flowers. Spices are used widely, making for a quirky twist on Venetian cuisine, such as in sardines with ginger.

Da Rioba

Fondamenta della Misericordia; tel: 041-524 4379; closed Mon; vaporetto: San Marcuola; €€

This rustic-chic restaurant is set on a canal that comes alive at night, and you can dine outside, by the bustling waterfront. The cooking is subtly creative, with pasta dishes or seafood, including tuna carpaccio.

Fiaschetteria Toscana

Salizzada San Giovanni Cristostomo; tel: 041-528 5281; closed all Tue, and Wed L; vaporetto: Rialto; €€€

Near the Rialto Bridge, this is a local favourite for excellent seafood, plus a smattering of Tuscan steak dishes and cheeses, and fine wines. Book.

Vini da Gigio

Fondamenta di San Felice; tel: 041-528 5140; closed Mon and Tue; vaporetto: Ca' d'Oro; €€

Cosy and romantic, this popular family-run inn serves reliable Slow Food with leisurely service. Lots of variety, from Venetian risotto to northern Italian game dishes. Book.

The Islands

Alla Maddalena

Fondamenta di Santa Caterina 7C, Mazzorbo; tel. 041-730 151; 8am–8pm; closed Thur; €€

At Burano, cross over the footbridge to Mazzorbo and enjoy a lazy seafood lunch in this authentic trattoria.

Al Ponte del Diavolo

Fondamenta Borgognoni 10, Isola di Torcello; tel: 041-730 401; L only; open Mar–Dec Tue–Sun; €€–€€€

A charming rustic lunch venue, with friendly guidance through the pasta and seafood menu.

Al Raspo De Ua

Via Galuppi 560, Isola di Burano; tel: 041-730 095; L only; €€

Tuck into excellent pasta with prawns on the main square in Burano.

Above from far left: dinner on Piazza San Marco; busy wine bar.

Island Eating
The outlying islands are home to some of Venice's most intriguing restaurants. Try Venezzia on Mazzorbo *(see Tour 12)* or, for a real adventure, take a water taxi or private boat to the little island of Le Vignole (it's not on a vaporetto route) and eat beneath the trees at the Trattoria alle Vignole (www.trattoriaalle vignole.com).

Venetian nightlife does exist but can feel like an insider secret until, probably after a *giro d'ombra* wine crawl and one prosecco too many, you crack the code. The traditional take on the city is that nightlife is low-key, focused on piano bars, the historic cafés around San Marco and chic hotel bars. This is true, but so is its opposite.

Your evening could begin with a toast to Venice, on the rooftop of **Terrazza Danieli** *(see p.111)*, admiring La Salute across the water. Or it could start in a rough-and-ready Rialto wine bar with a spritz and spicy sardines shared with off-duty gondoliers. But it's not a stark choice between the two: local people like to mix things up.

A Venetian elite may still meet to strains of Vivaldi at the fireside of a freshly gilded salon, but will also revel in a Dorsoduro neighbourhood bar, perhaps **Cantinone Gia Schiavi** (Fondamenta Nani, Dorsoduro 992; tel: 041-523 0034) where the creative *cicchetti* are at odds with the beaten-up interior. Or maybe settle for prosecco and a stroll on the Zattere waterfront. From there, it's a short hop over the Giudecca canal to the lofty heights of the **Skyline Rooftop Bar** (Molino Stucky Hilton, Fondamenta San Biagio 810; tel: 041-272 3311). Then with the summer sunset reflected in a peachy Bellini, it may be time to leave the Giudecca rooftops for a seafood supper in an authentic inn.

Mapping your mood

If planning a bar crawl, be influenced by neighbourhood, mood and personal taste for authenticity, tranquillity or live music. Depending on mood and means, you can opt for a nightlife scene that ranges from romantic to rakish, from sedate piano bar to stylish sushi bar, from buzzing Lido beach club to downbeat bohemian inn. And wine bars, whether 'new-wave' or traditional *bacari*, will be bursting with tasty treats to detain you from dinner.

Rumbustious Rialto

As a bazaar city, Venice was on the spice route, and the Rialto was at its heart. Latter-day merchants of Venice can still be encountered on a Rialto bar crawl. Known as a *giro d'ombra*, it is best begun at sunset as some of the more traditional bars close early. These time-warp taverns are the perfect introduction to *cicchetti*, from slivers of dried salt cod to tiny meatballs or sweet and sour sardines. The boisterous **Do Mori** (Calle de Do Mori; *see Walk 10*) has operated since 1462 so it is not inconceivable that Tintoretto was a patron. The artist would have approved of mixing with the populace, and eating *crostini* with salt cod or a paste of chicken liver and capers.

Venetians consider the *cicchetti* at **All'Arco** *(see Tour 14)* even better, where a father-son team mix creative and conservative creations. Nearby, the canalside Erberia has become the new meeting-place at cocktail hour. These bars tend to be new-wave *bacari* that look traditional but have dared to redesign the menu in tune with the times. **Muro** *(see Tour 2)* and **Bancogiro** *(see Walk 10)* feel both

contemporary yet faithful to the spirit of the old mercantile Rialto.

Bohemian Cannaregio

The bar crawl segues into bohemian Cannaregio, where you could begin with bustling **Taverna del Campiello Remer** *(see Walk 10; for directions see www.alremer.com)* for a Grand Canal view and tapas in an atmospheric vaulted inn (5.30–7.30pm), or come back later for live music or even dinner.

Closer to the Ca' d'Oro ferry stop, **Alla Vedova** (Ramo Ca' d'Oro; *see Tour 11*) is an engagingly old-world, cheap-and-cheerful *bacaro*. After fuelling yourself on authentic *cicchetti*, call into the neighbouring **Al Santo Bevitore** (Calle Zancani 239; tel: 041-717 560), a canalside corner awash with fans of Trappist ales. If hunger has got the better of you, feast on superb tapas at **La Cantina** (Campo San Felice; *see Tour 11*) or, if you prefer moody lagoon views, then traipse to **Algiubagio** on the Fondamenta Nuove quaysides (tel: 041-523 6084; *see Restaurants*). From the *bacaro* terrace let your eyes feast on San Michele cemetery island while you graze on creative *cicchetti* or tuck into dinner. Over towards the Ghetto is **Al Timon** (Fondamenta degli Ormesini; *see Tour 11*), a place for dreaming over organic DOC wines, and maybe catching some folk music. But if finding the Cannaregio quaysides a touch bleak, restore your spirits in **Paradiso Perduto** (Fondamenta de la Misericordia 2640; tel: 041-720 581), a bohemian live music haunt on a sleepy canalside that wakes up at night.

Glamorous San Marco

For old-school glamour, the water-front-hotel piano bars have been playing the same tune for centuries. But if you can resist the tinkling from these grande-dame bars, drink in a sunset view from the **Terrazza Danieli** *(see p.111)* before the bar criminally closes at 7pm. **Harry's Bar** *(see p.47)* may be a legend but the Danieli exudes old-school glamour.

For an artier waterside bar, call into the next *calle* to sip a prosecco on the pontoon at **Ca' Giustinian** (Calle del Ridotto), a Gothic palace with sweeping views over to La Salute. Now the headquarters of the Biennale, it was once the hotel where Turner, Proust and Verdi all found artistic inspiration.

Arty partying also awaits further down the Grand Canal in a vision of Venice beloved by the celebrity set. **Palazzina Grassi** is home to several modish bars, where a Philippe Starck makeover has created a clubby look, with quirky Murano chandeliers and animal artworks in Carnival masks.

The celebrity set also feel utterly at home in the **B-Bar** (L'Hotel Bauer, Campo San Moise; tel: 041-520 7022), where the gold mosaics reflect the glitterati in all their glory.

Finally, for a taste of Manhattan-with-gondola-attached, you could call it a night at **Caffè Centrale** *(see p.117)* if only to conclude that, contrary to rumour, glamorous, night-owl Venice *does* indeed exist. Definitely go for the full-on Manhattan here, not a Venetian spritz.

Above: the bright lights of Piazza San Marco at night; local wines are divine.

Youth Haunts
Despite Venice's ageing population, Campo Santa Margherita is awash with buzzing, youth-oriented bars, of which Margaret Duchamp *(see Tour 7)* is the most sophisticated, but all have their fans.

Lido Beach Clubs
In summer, the Lido has its own youthful nightlife scene, not so much in the seafront grand hotels, but in the beach clubs. While many come and go, the Aurora *(see Tour 13)* is currently the most popular, with the latest DJs and cocktails winning over both Venetians and visitors.

CREDITS

Insight Step by Step Venice
Written by: Lisa Gerard-Sharp, Susie Boulton
and Jessica Stewart
Commissioning Editor: Siân Lezard
Series Editor: Carine Tracanelli
Cartography Editors: James Macdonald
Picture Manager: Yoshimi Kanazawa
Art Editor: Lucy Johnston
Production: Tynan Dean
Photography: All pictures Chris Coe/Apa Publications, Glyn Genin/Apa Publications, Mockford & Bonetti/Apa Publications except Alamy 7B, 10B, 16T, 18T, 18/19, 30B, 31TR, 32B, 32T, 38/39, 47, 49, 51, 52, 53B, 54, 55T, 55CR, 56, 57, 58TR, 59, 60, 64, 66TL, 67TR, 69, 71, 73, 75TR, 76T&B, 82, 91B, 112/113, 115, 116, 117, 120; Bigstock 12B, 104, 107; Bridgeman Art Library 44B; Neil Buchan-Grant/Apa Publications 38TL; Corbis 7CR; Dreamstime 2BL, 2TC, 4T, 4C, 11TR, 13, 15B, 29, 30T, 80TL, 81BR, 84, 96, 97, 102, 106; Getty Images 2/3, 6CL, 7T, 8/9, 10L, 12/13, 15T, 17R, 19, 20, 20/21, 21, 23, 24, 26/27, 33, 35T, 37, 41T&B, 42, 44/45, 46, 61T&B, 62, 63B, 68, 70, 72B, 74CT, 77T, 79TL, 81BL, 85, 86, 88/89, 90/91, 92T, 93,113TR, 114, 122; Robert Harding 94/95; iStockphoto 2BR, 2BC, 2TR, 2TL, 6TL, 11C, 14, 16CL, 22, 29TR, 30/31, 34, 35B, 36T, 39TR, 58TL, 72T, 79TR, 81TR; Britta Jaschinski/Apa Publications 118; Mary Evans 69B; Ros Miller 83T; Susan Smart/Apa Publications 123.
Front cover: main image: 4 Corners; bottom left and right: iStockphoto.
Back cover: left: iStockphoto; right: Bigstock.
Printed in China by: CTPS

www.insightguides.com

DISTRIBUTION

Worldwide
**APA Publications GmbH & Co. Verlag KG
(Singapore branch)**
7030 Ang Mo Kio Ave 5
08-65 Northstar @ AMK, Singapore 569880
Email: apasin@singnet.com.sg

UK and Ireland
**Dorling Kindersley Ltd
(a Penguin Company)**
80 Strand, London, WC2R 0RL, UK
Email: customerservice@uk.dk.com

United States
Ingram Publisher Services
One Ingram Blvd, PO Box 3006
La Vergne, TN 37086-1986
Email: customer.service@ingrampublisher
services.com

Australia
Universal Publishers
PO Box 307
St. Leonards NSW 1590
Email: sales@universalpublishers.com.au

New Zealand
Brown Knows Publications
11 Artesia Close, Shamrock Park
Auckland, New Zealand 2016
Email: sales@brownknows.co.nz

CONTACTING THE EDITORS

We would appreciate it if readers would alert us to errors or outdated information by writing to us at insight@apaguide.co.uk or APA Publications, PO Box 7910, London SE1 1WE, UK.

THE WORLD OF
INSIGHT GUIDES

Different people need different kinds of travel information.
Some want background facts. Others seek personal
recommendations. With a variety of different products – Insight
Guides, Insight City Guides, Step by Step Guides, Smart Guides,
Insight Fleximaps and our new Great Breaks series –
we offer readers the perfect choice.

Insight Guides will turn your visit into an experience.

www.insightguides.com

INDEX

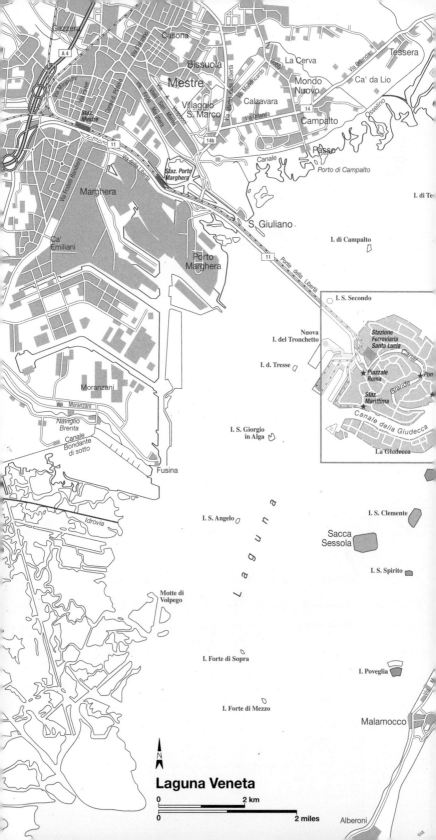